THINK LIKE A LEADER

150 Top Business Leaders
Show You How Their Minds Work

Dr Harry Alder

PIATKUS

To Gloria

First published in 1995
by Judy Piatkus (Publishers) Ltd
5 Windmill Street, London W1P 1HF

First paperback edition 1996

The moral rights of the author have been asserted

*A catalogue record for this book is available
from the British Library*

ISBN 0-7499-1479-3 (Hbk)
ISBN 0-7499-1612-5 (Pbk)

Data manipulation by
Phoenix Photosetting, Chatham, Kent
Printed and bound in Great Britain by
Mackays of Chatham PLC

Contents

About the Leaders

DURING THE COURSE of writing this book I interviewed more than 150 leaders of British companies – almost all chairmen and chief executives. Some I met more than once, with meetings extending up to half a day. More than half of those interviewed headed companies in the top 200 of *The Times* 1000 listing, responsible together for many billions of pounds of turnover – a sizeable chunk of the national economy. The remainder represented a wide range of medium and smaller companies.

Those interviewed have nothing in common that I am aware of, other than being in a top leadership role, and happening to agree to help with my research, so presumably have some interest in the subject of leadership. They would not necessarily subscribe to my views, or to those of their colleagues in other companies, that appear throughout the book. Those contributing are listed in alphabetical order, with their position and company at the time of the interview. Some have retired or changed companies since. Relatively few of those listed are quoted by name in the book. This is not because they had nothing meaningful to say – quite the contrary – but because the common themes and experiences that emerged could be well illustrated without quoting every leader. So views and anecdotes are representative rather than exhaustive, and are certainly no reflection of quality of leadership – the leadership credentials of every one of those contributing is self-evident from their actual role. It is therefore all the more important for me to thank everyone listed below who gave their time, in some cases reviewing detailed manuscript. I must also thank the anonymous secretaries and PAs who juggled diaries to make possible more than 200 interviews.

THE CONTRIBUTORS

John Aldridge	Chairman & Managing Director	Leicester Mercury Group
Sir David Alliance	Chairman	Coats Viyella
Robert Ayling	Group Managing Director	British Airways
John Baker	Chief Executive	National Power
Frank Barlow	Managing Director	Pearson
Don Bennett	Joint Managing Director	Texaco Ltd
Lilian Bennett	Chairman	Manpower
Peter Bennett	Group Managing Partner	Howes Percival
Mike Bett	Deputy Chairman	British Telecom
John Billing	Executive Director	Courtaulds Textiles
John Blake	Managing Director	Angus Fire Armour
John Bourke	Chief Executive	TSB Commercial Holdings
Jonathan Bowman	Managing Director	Berol
Sir Keith Bright	former Chairman	Brent Walker Group
John Browne	Chief Executive Officer	BP Exploration
Hamish Bryce	Executive Chairman	Thorn Lighting Group (TLG Plc)
Alan Buckle	former Managing Director	BRS Automotive
	(now Deputy Director, Exel Logistics)	
Chris Bucknall	Managing Director	Compass Services (UK)
Robert Burlton	Chief Executive	Oxford, Swindon & Glouc Co-op
Roger Burnell	Managing Director	Britannia Airways
Andrew Buxton	Chairman	Barclays Bank
Robert Campbell	Chief Executive	Platignum
Geoffrey Cardinal	Chairman	Mobil Oil Company
John Carter	Group Chief Executive	Hepworth
Bryan Castledine	Chairman & Chief Executive	Erith
Robin Chudley	Chairman	Foilwraps Flexible Packaging
Neil Clarke	Chairman	British Coal Corporation

Sir Anthony Cleaver	former Chairman	IBM UK
	(now Chairman, AEA Technology)	
John G Collier	Chairman	Nuclear Electric
John Conlan	Chief Executive	First Leisure Corporation
Graham Cooper	former Managing Director	Autotype International (Norcros)
Douglas Corbishley	Group Vice President	National Starch & Chemical
Barry Dale	Group Chief Executive	The Littlewoods Organisation
John Dale	Managing Director	Pedigree Petfoods
Paul Damoc	former Managing Director	Federal Express Europe
Michael Dandy	Managing Director	Gibbs & Dandy
Frank Davies	former Chairman	Rockware Group
Peter Davis	former Chairman	Reed International
Julian Dell	Group Managing Director	Strong & Fisher
Richard Dick	Managing Director	W Lucy & Co
Ebbe Dinesen	Chief Executive	Carlsberg-Tetley Brewing
Ian Dixon	Chairman	Willmott Dixon
Keith Dixon	former Managing Director	Triton
Peter Douglas	Managing Partner	Kidsons Impey
Derek Drake	Managing Director	Servowarm Heating Service
Les Dunn	Managing Director	Crabtree Electrical Industries
Rodney East	Group Managing Director	Etam
Peter Ellwood	Chief Executive	TSB Group
Sir Robert Evans	former Chairman	British Gas
Malcolm Farrar	Managing Director	Coats
Sir Malcolm Field	Group Chief Executive	W H Smith
Sir Rocco Forte	Chairman	Forte
Len Fyfe	Chairman	CWS
Simon Flude	Director	H Flude & Co
Andrew Freeman	Chief Executive	Atkins Group
Sir Anthony Gill	former Chairman & Chief Exec	Lucas Industries
Sir Paul Girolami	former Chairman	Glaxo
Richard Gooding	Chief Executive	London Luton Airport
Sir Nicholas Goodison	Chairman	TSB Bank
Ted Goold	former Managing Director	Triton
Irene Graham	Managing Director	Target Life Assurance Co
Sir Richard Greenbury	Chairman	Marks & Spencer
Clive Groom	Managing Director	Matthew Hall
Tim Harford	Managing Director	Europcar UK

Mike Harris	former Chief Executive	Mercury Communications
Dr Robert Hawley	Chief Executive	Nuclear Electric
Sir Denys Henderson	Chairman	ICI and Zencca
Jeffrey Herbert	Chief Executive	Charter plc
Leslie Hill	Managing Director	Central Independent TV
John Hoerner	Chief Executive	The Burton Group
Sir Simon Hornby	former Chairman	W H Smith
	(now Chairman, Lloyds Abbey Life)	
Sir John Hoskyns	Chairman	The Burton Group
Tony Howard	Managing Director	Brook Street
Colin Howell	Group Managing Director	Bostram
Sipko Huismans	Chief Executive	Courtaulds
Brian Husselbee	Managing Director, Europe	NCH Promotional Services
Richard Ide	Managing Director	VAG (UK)
Mike Illsley	Managing Director	P P Payne (Norcros)
John Jackson	Deputy Chairman	Hillsdown Holdings
Mike Jackson	Chief Executive	Birmingham Midshires Building Soc
Peter Jacobs	Chief Executive	BUPA
Clem Jansen	Group Managing Director	Silvermines Group
Stanley Kalms	Chairman	Dixon Group
Iain Kennedy	Joint Managing Director	Church & Co
Leon King	Managing Director	Fosroc Expandite
Martin Laing	Chairman	John Laing
Robert Lawson	Group Chief Executive	Electrocomponents
Vincent Lawton	Managing Director	Merck Sharp & Dohme
Paul Lester	Managing Director	Graseby
Marion Lewis	Director of Marketing	Logica International
Dr M R Lloyd	Managing Director	GEC Alsthom Traction
David Lyon	Managing Director & Chief Exec	Bowater
Brian Maguire	Managing Director	Golden West Foods
Leszec Marcinowicz	Vice President Human Resources	Parker Hannifin
Charles Mackay	Chief Executive	Inchcape
Robert McKinley	former Chairman	British Aerospace
Andrew Michel	Managing Director	FKI Babcock
David Moore	Managing Director	BICC Transmitton
Terry Moore	Chief Executive Officer	Conoco
Wayne Murcar	former Managing Director	British Pipeline Agency

Dr Peter Nevitt	former Managing Director	Cosworth Engineering
John Newman	Commercial Director	Shanks & McEwan Group
Bob Nice	Managing Director	Ratcliff Tail Lifts
Archie Norman	Chairman	Asda Group
Keith Oates	Deputy Chairman & MD	Marks & Spencer
David Oldroyd	former Managing Director	Arlington Motor Co
Lou O'Toole	Managing Director	Beans Industries
Alan Padgett	Managing Director	Mettler-Toledo
Tony Palmer	Chief Executive	Taylor Woodrow
Dr Frieder Paascha	Managing Director	Brose
David Peake	Exec Group Chairman	Kleinwort Benson Group
Sir Brian Pearse	former Director & Chief Exec (now Chairman, Lucas Industries)	Midland Bank
Jurek Piasecki	Chief Executive	Goldsmiths Group
Stefan Pijanowski	Managing Director	DuBois
Douglas Pirie	Managing Director	Kenchington Ford
Steven Poster	Managing Director	Granada
Pat Prendergast	Managing Director	Autobar
David A Quarmby	Joint Managing Director	J Sainsbury
Grant Rabey	Managing Director	RS Components
Roy Ranson	Managing Director & Actuary	Equitable Life Assurance Society
Sir Ralph Robins	Chairman	Rolls Royce
Andrew Robinson	Managing Director	Gent
Michael Rouse	Deputy Chairman	WRc
Jack Rowell	former Chief Executive (and Manager, England rugby union team)	Golden Wonder
Vernon L Sankey	Chief Executive	Reckitt & Colman
Graham Scott	Managing Director	McKilroys (Courtaulds Textiles)
Trevor Sculthorpe-Pike	Director & GM	Viking Johnson
Sir Neil Shaw	Executive Chairman	Tate & Lyle
David Shingler	Managing Director	Unistrut (UK)
Len Simmonds	Managing Director	T Bailey Forman
Fred Simons	Senior VP & GM UK	Manulife
Ian Smith	Managing Director	Lunn Poly
Dr Jim Smith	Chairman	Eastern Electricity Group
Peter Smith	Managing Director	Marconi Instruments
Robert Solberg	Deputy Chairman	Texaco
Sir Colin Southgate	Chairman	THORN EMI

Paul Southworth	President	Avon Cosmetics
John Sunderland	Managing Director	Cadbury/Schweppes Group Confectionary
Jerry Swan	Managing Director	Caterpillar UK
Michael Switzer	former Regional Chairman (now Marketing Director, British Gas, Retail)	British Gas, East Midlands
Sir Richard Sykes	Deputy Chairman & Chief Exec	Glaxo
Nick Temple	Chairman	IBM UK
Ian Thomson	Managing Director	British Shoe Corporation
Michael Travis	former Chief Executive	Heart of England Building Soc
David Tucker	Chairman & Managing Director	BeWise
Frank Turner	Managing Director	Lucas Aerospace Industries
David Varney	Joint Managing Director	Shell UK
Charles Villiers	Managing Director Corp. Dev.	Abbey National
Tom Vyner	Deputy Chairman & Joint M D	J Sainsbury
Ed Wallis	Chief Executive	PowerGen
Piet Walton-Knight	Managing Director	Dunlop (Aircraft Tyres)
Mark Warland	Managing Director	Irvin (G B)
Timothy Waterstone	Chief Executive	Waterstone Booksellers
David Watkins	Managing Director	Lucas Hartridge
David Webster	Deputy Chairman	Argyll Group
John Welsby	Chief Executive	British Rail
Michael Wemms	Retail Director	Tesco
Ken Whittaker	Managing Director	Hoogovens Steel
Derek Williams	Managing Director	Coca Cola Schweppes (CCSB)
Paul Williams	Managing Director	Bristol Street Motors
Tony Wilkinson	Chairman	Wilkinson Group
David Wilson	Chairman & Chief Executive	Wilson Bowden
Robert Wilson	Chief Executive	RTZ Corporation
Anders Wincent	former Chairman & Chief Exec	CSE Aviation
Chris Winn	former Managing Director	ACT Computer Support
Grahame Winter	Group Managing Director	Maples Group
Tony Withey	Chief Executive	Remploy
John Woodgate	Managing Director	Oxford Magnet Technology
Lord Young	Chairman	Cable & Wireless

(Positions as at time of interview.)

What's so Special about a Leader?

EACH OF US has the capacity to be a leader. Many of us already lead a family, group or team of some sort, and we can of course be leaders through our ideas and influence, besides being a boss in a formal hierarchy. For most of us, however, although we see political and other leaders on our television screens, our main contact with leaders is in the workplace. This book looks particularly at business leaders who head up organisations – in some cases, very large ones. Most of the company bosses interviewed agreed that leaders are made, not born. Some had well-formed views of what leadership is all about, and these are shared with you throughout the book. As we shall see, not only are the lessons from these business leaders common to leadership generally, they are also simple enough for any of us to learn and follow.

SOMEONE WHO PEOPLE TEND TO FOLLOW

You don't get to run a multi-billion pound company, commanding the respect of thousands of people – many with technical and professional skills that make the leader look quite amateur by comparison – by being just one of the crowd. A leader is someone who people tend to follow. To command a following – a willing following – the leader has to do something, or be something, that *makes* people follow. There has to be something that inspires trust, respect, or admiration, even though, as followers, we cannot readily identify what it is. What makes an ordinary person special, what makes a manager a leader, and what explains the apparent mystique surrounding those who make it to the top is a difference; and, whatever the difference is, it must be significant. That difference is what this book is all about.

Fostering creative leadership is not just a matter of skills and techniques – that's why so many managers miss the mark of true leadership. And that's what makes this book different – it doesn't offer new techniques, or a grand theory. It's not that theories and techniques are not useful – they are valuable enough. But most of us know that, even when we use the latest methods, or follow neat models, there is still something missing. Sometimes, despite all the training and advice from gurus, we might even think we are going backwards. Techniques certainly do *not* create a leader – you cannot train a leader as you can a book-keeper or machinist.

There remains an underlying mystique about the whole subject. What takes place when we experience excellence in any field is sometimes beyond our understanding and control – beyond our awareness even. What makes an entertainer a star, a sportsperson a true champion, or a politician a statesman? People can adopt an unconscious mode of competence that cannot be fully explained by knowledge, skill, or intelligence. The things you are really good at seem natural to you, and you don't see why others make a fuss about it. We see this in top sports people and artists as well as scientists or outstanding business leaders. They seem to occupy a different plane, to have tapped into a different dimension. But their secrets are not apparent from analysis. Rather than analysing the parts, such as skills or personality traits, we have to look at leaders in a new way that sees the whole – the total person.

For all this apparent mystique, the skills, attitudes and lifestyle that I found were central to the success of leaders are common to us all in different degrees. But the leaders I met happen to have applied themselves towards leadership and business goals, rather than to other areas in which others excel. So, although my research featured some of the top earners in the country, and leaders of industry and commerce, I found that what gives them the edge is not a super brain or special genes. Much of what I learned can be applied by ordinary people. These leaders are ordinary in every way, except for what I have identified as a special edge, comprising simple factors that are easily missed by managers climbing single-mindedly towards the top.

REMOVING THE MYSTIQUE OF LEADERSHIP

So, are leaders that special? Lord Young, now chairman of Cable and Wireless and one time member of Mrs Thatcher's cabinet, uses a telling analogy about leadership and personal power. He describes how, on entering secondary school, he was in awe of the fifth-formers. They seemed to occupy a higher level of knowledge and wisdom, seemingly out of the reach of lesser mortals. But on rising through each school year, with its increasing status and influence, and in due course entering the ranks of the fifth form himself, he was surprised to find that his contemporaries were very ordinary, if not mediocre. They turned out not to be the gods that fifth-formers had seemed to be, and he was happy to hold his own against any of them. As his career progressed throughout industry and commerce, he was to find, time and time again, that people in positions of leadership only seem special from a distance. First on becoming a manager, then a managing director, his earlier perceptions were quickly dispelled as he found the same mediocrity he had on reaching the fifth form. The analogy – which most of us can immediately relate to – was further reinforced for David Young when, in the mid-Eighties, he joined the cabinet of Margaret Thatcher, which was replete with the political heavyweights he had previously seen only from the relative anonymity of business life. The dizzy heights of political leadership were not what they had seemed from a distance – it was like joining the fifth form all over again!

NEW PERSPECTIVES ON LEADERSHIP

So much has changed during the second half of the 20th century that it has become a tedious requirement of any serious economic, political or business study to recount all the details of technological and social upheaval, from the ubiquitous microchip to the demise of communism. Few areas of knowledge have escaped being turned upside down. The only certainty for tomorrow's managers is still more change. Management science, however, has not advanced at the same pace as other areas of science and technology – at least not from where I have sat as a practising manager or trainer. This is not to say we have been short of buzz concepts and panaceas. But in most cases the new flavour of the year turns out to be either repackaged common sense that any middle manager could have proposed – just wishing he or she had invented the jargon words – or a neat formula for excellence that simply did not work outside the factory, industry, or country where it apparently worked for some-body else. So some new perspectives are overdue.

It seems that it is the less tangible characteristics of lead-ership – rather than structures, systems, and strategies – which account for the important 'difference that makes the difference'. You have got to know these characteristics if you are to understand what leadership is – let alone become a leader.

Using both sides of the brain

Henry Mintzberg, whilst observing what managers actually did, recognised that the enormously complex, key manager-ial processes 'seem to be most characteristic of right brain hemispheric activity'. My book *The Right Brain Manager* (Piatkus) explored the way in which the creative, intuitive right brain as well as the logical, rational left brain are both important for a manager's effectiveness. I went on to show just how the right brain can be harnessed to bring about quantum rather than merely incremental improvements in a manager's performance. It remained, then, to find out more about what the best managers do, and also how they think – in particular how, when, and to what effect they use both sides of the brain. I wanted to know what these people actu-ally do that exhibits the 'passion', 'courage' and other traits that have been linked to excellent leadership.

The role of analysis, formal planning and systems has been well covered in other writings. I wanted to learn at first hand what part intuition and so-called gut feelings play in the lives of top business leaders. As well as *The Right Brain Manager*, my more recent book on the subject of neuro-lin-guistic programming (NLP) explored these subjects, draw-ing on our knowledge of the working of the brain and important developments in psychology and human achievement. Work involving attitude and mental approach in sports coaching, for example, tends to be ahead of applications in management science.

Sir Geoffrey Chandler, former director-general of NEDO, refers to the need for intuition as well as analysis, especially in dealings with people: 'Since it is failures in human relationships, perhaps more than failures in analysis (which you can at the end of the day buy in), that lead to business disasters, it could make sense to ensure that no manager reaches a top position without exposure to such training.'

I added an important new feature to this study of leadership. I talked with business leaders as *people* – total persons with a life outside the corporation, however demanding their business role. Best described as an holistic approach, this brought interesting insights into how top leaders lead.

Who is a leader?

There is bound to be disagreement about whether the leaders I interviewed are good leaders, or the best models for those aspiring to higher things. Questions could also be raised as to how British industry and commerce has performed, under their leadership, as compared with other competitor countries. I have avoided such controversy. For better or worse, these chairmen and CEOs happen to occupy the seats of power. They *are* our business leaders. My research suggests why they, and not other people, are sitting there. The fact that they are leaders speaks for itself, in the sheer size and complexity of the businesses they have led, in some cases for many years. Many are responsible for tens of thousands of staff. I spent a morning with Michael Wemms at Tesco who, as director of retail activities (and neither chairman nor CEO), has about *one hundred thousand* people to lead. Keith Oates at Marks & Spencer is responsible for more stores than the number of staff that most managing directors head up. Even those running smaller companies, who I included to give a sufficiently wide representation, qualify as leaders for the purpose of this book. Without doubt, some of them will be leading the mega-corporations of the future.

Managers and leaders

Some leadership textbooks labour over the distinction between a manager and a leader. I do not spend time on this distinction, nor do I try to define them respectively. There are plenty of middle or senior 'managers' in large companies who have a bigger 'followership' than many chief executives, and many of the top executives I met have some boss or other themselves. I am happy to call them all top managers. You can't be a good manager – of a team, a department, or an organisation – without being a leader, although the leadership dimension becomes more important as the number of followers and size of organisation increases. It is the leadership part of management that I address.

Sir Peter Parker, former chairman of British Rail and a student and practitioner of leadership, also refutes the manager/leader distinction, whilst confirming what I have found – that there are many ways to lead (and manage). It boils down to how the manager thinks. Whilst Henry Mintzberg differentiated between the leader and the manager, his distinctions were almost wholly related to the left-brain right-brain differences I and others have identified as crucial to thinking and behaviour. For instance, as he sees it:

- the manager administrates – the leader innovates
- the manager imitates – the leader originates

● the manager accepts the status quo – the leader challenges it

and so on. It quickly becomes apparent that a manager cannot ignore the leadership aspects of his role. And it is this
critical element of true leadership that this research was
aimed at. Being stuck with the two terms, I prefer to distin-
guish simply between good and bad leaders, or good and
bad managers.

Outside the corridors of power

My research for this book was not confined to the boardroom or company offices. Nor was it confined to 'office
hours' – however abnormal they may be in the case of a
leading chairman or chief executive. Leaders might be seen
grappling with strategic issues or a nagging personnel issue
whilst sailing alone on a favourite waterway, waking in the
small hours of the morning with a million pounds' worth of
ideas, or perhaps a ready-made speech or report, or sharing
a chance conversation whilst on holiday, resulting in a major
company innovation. These personal insights, and the sort
of lifestyle that fosters them, tell us a lot about the leaders
and how they lead.

Business leaders

I specifically restricted my interviews to business leaders. Sir
Peter Parker argues that managing a business is different
from a military command, or political or religious leadership – a business tycoon has neither electoral nor divine
rights. He has to establish his own legitimacy, and the question inevitably is raised: 'Why should people follow?' Top
managers in industry and commerce, however varied their
personalities and roles, do represent what most of us,

mainly as employees, see as leaders. As it happens, some of the leaders I interviewed occupy, or have occupied, leadership roles in other areas, such as politics or sport, besides in business. Jack Rowell, for example, managed at the time of our meeting not just Golden Wonder but also the England rugby union squad. So I was able to compare common factors, as well as differences, in getting at some of their secrets of leadership success.

My earlier work drew on a far wider population of leaders. Neuro-linguistic programming, for example, has 'modelled' personal excellence in a whole range of fields. And my work as a management trainer over the years allows me to draw on the experience of hundreds of managers, many practising outside of industry and commerce. But regardless of the field in which you aspire to be a leader, the fundamental features of leadership that my research has uncovered will be of help.

The real leader has an edge, especially when measured over the longer term. Not only can we identify this edge, but it turns out that – just like entering the fifth form – it's no big deal. These people have standard brains and just a fair ration of natural abilities, but they use them in a special way. *That's* what makes a leader special.

In the next chapter I explore what is going on *inside* the leader – his thinking style and beliefs, and the importance of what he *is* rather than just what he *does*, or seems to do. (To avoid undue repetition and contrived grammar I use the masculine pronoun from time to time to include men and women, although the preponderance of male business leaders is, in any event, a sad reality). In Chapter 3 I show the part that intuition plays in the lives of leaders, how they get a good flow of ideas and keep a fresh mind. Chapter 4 takes us further into the minds of the leaders, examining how they think, for example in solving problems and making decisions. In particular, Chapter 4 looks at the different kinds of thought, the stages involved, and the significance of these in the leader's success. Here we cover creative problem solving, what it means to 'sleep on a problem', and how the leader faces up to difficult, urgent decisions. In Chapter 5 we see the leader from a wider perspective, for example, how he relates work and leisure, and how non-work time and private life impact on his leadership and on the business.

One chief executive I met remarked how he thought Margaret Thatcher, the former British prime minister, had lost touch with ordinary people towards the end of her premiership. Chapter 6 looks at how leaders keep in touch, both within their company, and with the world at large, and how this affects their effectiveness as leaders. We shall see, however, that this concerns more than management style and staff relations, and relates to how the leader thinks, and what goes on inside, as covered in the earlier chapters. Choosing good people – vital for any leader – is more an art than a science. This is covered in Chapter 7. The people part of leadership was central to all the research, and the wider aspects of this, including the topical 'empowerment' of people, are also addressed in this chapter. In the absence of a master theory or neat model of leadership success, I attempt in the last chapter to draw a pattern from all the contributions of the leaders, and to translate this into what you can do to become a true leader.

To make this book especially practical, at the end of each chapter I suggest 'tips for tomorrow's leaders'. Follow these on a day to day basis – without thinking about it, you will start to think like a leader.

2

Leading from the Inside

WHAT MAKES a successful leader? Having chosen some examples of top leaders, what should we look for? According to the textbooks, what you accomplish in leadership or anything else depends upon what you *do* – it is hard to dispute this simple cause-and-effect relationship. Very few of the leaders I met attributed their success to luck – nor, as it happened, to genetics, education or a privileged background. Even the luck argument for success demands that you get to be in the right places at the right time now and again and do the sort of things that are likely to bring results. In other words, you make your own luck. You have got to perform – produce the goods – if you are to be more than a nine-day wonder. If you are fortunate enough to have had a genetic running start – fine. But you have to do something with it. Even the most basic natural skills have to be used and developed. That's why most leadership books focus on behaviour.

LEADERSHIP STYLE AND TRAITS

But that is just the start. Leadership traits have been investigated over many years. Scores have been identified – from IQ to physical height. Only wings are missing. Style also became fashionable a few years ago, so we started labelling the auto-crats (Theory X) and the nice consensus types (Theory Y), the tellers and the askers. Whilst each successive theory has seemed more plausible, as is the tendency with theories, we are still a long way from accounting for success in leadership. People with all the traits were nowhere to be found. And those with the basic qualities like intelligence are everywhere – yet few are leaders. Obviously you need to be fairly bright, if some or all of your followers are bright. But then you also need intelligence to hold down a technical job with no staff reporting to you, or to handle the family budget.

Alongside intelligence, people skills rank high in popular leadership traits. But some salespeople exhibit outstanding interpersonal skills, are also intelligent, yet are not leaders. The autocratic managers first spawned by the industrial revolution are supposed to be a thing of the past in our enlightened society. But among the masses of enlightened, democratic managers, precious few real leaders seem to emerge.

So much for leadership behaviour in the form of style and traits. Specific traits, style, or a magical mixture of them, have not provided the answer to 'What makes a good leader?' – let alone 'How can I become a leader?' Among the leaders I personally interviewed, many did not fit outward leadership traits, and I continued to search for something more funda-mental. The answer seemed to be more to do with who the leader *was* – the sort of person, his values and beliefs, how he ticked, what motivated him – rather than just what he did.

WHAT DOES A LEADER *DO*?

In observing particular activities, it is sometimes obvious who has 'got it' and who hasn't. A company chairman, for example, might be able to deliver a brilliant impromptu speech, or a sportsperson effortlessly accomplish what for most of us is impossible. In the case of the sportsperson, excellence relates to a particular skill, or a relatively narrow range of skills, although what might be called a 'champion's mentality', or 'star quality' in a performer, might equate to the leader's charisma. But it is less certain that the chairman's speech-making skills equate to good leadership.

Excellence in leadership embraces a wide range of factors. So, in terms of *behaviour*, the whole approach to 'how to be a leader' needs to be very different from 'how to be a public speaker' (or tennis player or book-keeper). Which parts of the leader do we have to copy? Is what a leader *does* the secret of his leadership? 'Charisma' or 'presence' are the terms often cited as leadership characteristics. But what does a leader actually *do* that displays these mysterious, elusive qualities? Is there a visible part of the iceberg that can tell us something about the leader's secrets? Where do outward skills and behaviour fit?

If one-to-one personal communication, say, happens to be a bigger factor in leadership success than public oratory, or perhaps mental arithmetic, many naturally outgoing people would see themselves rating high, and thus having the makings of a leader. At worst we would know where to concentrate our training and development. It makes sense that certain activities will be more important than others. Some, it would seem, are vital, because by their nature – like choosing and leading your immediate team, and making final decisions – you cannot delegate these activities; the buck has to stop somewhere. Keeping in touch with people in the company, for example, must also rank high in the leader's core requirements. But, when 'keeping in touch' is done well, it seems to be more to do with the leader's values about people, and beliefs about the very nature of his role, than with any professional communication skill, however polished. That is, it is to do with *how the leader thinks*. So, having identified the important behaviours – like keeping in touch, choosing good people, or making sound decisions - we need then to know what attitudes, beliefs or thought processes underlie these behaviours and the leader's consequent success.

Two managing directors give the same speech to their assembled staff in more or less the same way – with all the intonation, pauses and gesticulations any public presenter has to employ. Objectively, you or I might score them evenly. But the *effect* of one might be completely different from the other. In one case the staff are rallied to further effort and go away highly motivated. In the other case there is scepticism or disbelief, and accusations of whitewashing or hypocrisy or worse; the whole event backfires and any respect is lost. A trained practitioner in neuro-linguistic programming, or an expert in body language, might well be able to spot the non-verbal nuances that accounted for the difference. But that's a hard way to get at the secrets of leadership. Something *behind* the behaviour, or outward skill, will usually account for the very different outcomes.

Identifying what makes the difference

How can we identify the important difference? In all probability, there *were* major differences between the two managing directors who gave the same speech. Not in outward behaviour, but in their attitude, values, feelings and beliefs – in the way they were thinking. Beliefs tend to 'come through'. There has to be congruence between what we think and what we do. And the thinking – in a very wide sense, that includes attitude and belief – comes first. Even in sport, especially at the top, mental attitude seems to tip the balance in eventual success. We cannot readily identify, let alone analyse and emulate, the self-image and feelings that underlie human behaviour. When we do – and this is an area in which neuro-lingustic programming has brought outstanding results - we begin to understand the difference between competence and excellence, or how a manager emerges as a leader.

In this book I have concentrated on these aspects of the leader, which may not be readily observable. Some researchers have chosen a handful of outstanding 'celebrity' leaders, and followed them on their daily rounds like time and motion technicians. I have drawn on a large number of top business leaders, and informally discussed what is behind their leadership success. The quality of the answers I got made up for the naivety of my early questions: 'Where do you get your ideas?' ('Rarely in the office or board-room'.) 'Does intuition play a part?' ('. . . massive reliance on my intuition.') 'What do you believe about the company (never mind the mission statement), and yourself?' ('I just knew we could be number one.') 'How do you view work and leisure?' Some of these business leaders had never pre-viously even discussed these aspects of their thinking, and gained insights in the interview. The non-business side of their leadership success, in particular, had rarely been reflected upon, let alone divulged. Lifestyle quickly became a bigger factor in my volumes of notes than corporate struc-ture or communication systems. Imagination and intuition, once given credibility in serious research, held their own against analysis, formal planning processes, and the strait-jacket of left-brain bureaucracy.

It is the thinking and attitudes behind behaviour that prove to be the critical differences – the differences that give the leaders a special edge. Style, traits, or a portfolio of lead-ership skills leave the aspiring leader more confused than helped and motivated. The leader's life took on significance outside the business, and at weekends rather than during office hours. Simple anecdotes revealed a lot about the values and lifestyle that accompany success. Some of the mystique surrounding what leaders do, and the 'fifth form' awe in which they have been held over the years, was peeled away.

WHAT YOU DO WITH YOUR BRAIN

The leader is a thinker. Not, perhaps, in the cerebral way we usually associate with academics, or 'boffins'; but leaders are bright; they use their minds. Physical excellence was never an important part of management. The top of the management ladder calls for *bicameral* brainpower – calling on right brain power, as well as the familiar left brain analytical thinking which is where the academic or business analyst might excel. And that means leaders are imaginative, intuitive, perceptive, and creative, producing quality ideas, as well as hunches, insights and the 'eurekas', or flashes of inspiration that seem so different from ordinary, deliberate thinking.

But the creative right brain has had a bad press. Instincts are not often admitted as the basis of decisions in the modern boardroom. And 'gut feelings' have been more associated with win-some-lose-some, self-made entrepreneurs than professional corporate directors. MBA syllabuses and management textbooks do not reflect the reality of what leaders do and how they think. This, however, is how they *do* think, and it applies more at this level than to the ranks of middle management.

It's how you *use* your brain that is important. The hardware is standard – about 3½ pounds in weight. The heaviest recorded human brain in Britain was that of an Edinburgh man who died at the age of 75 in a hospital for the insane. On the other hand there was a young student at Sheffield

University who had an IQ of 126, gained a first class honours degree in mathematics, and was socially completely normal. But instead of the normal 4.5 centimetres of brain tissue, a brain scan found there was just a thin layer measuring about a millimetre deep. His cranium, according to a conference address, was 'filled mainly with cerebrospinal fluid'. So much for brain hardware. It's what we do with it that counts.

USING INTUITION AND CREATIVITY

One reason for the massive cooperation I received from household name business leaders was an immediate recognition on their part of the significance of intuition and creativity in leadership success. Many leaders are using daily what to them is a sort of sixth sense. But because such irrationality does not fit the neat analytical models of management science, it has remained unarticulated or positively frowned upon. The logical, verbal left side of the brain has long been known as the dominant side. The right side (linked as it is to the left hand, with all its negative connotations) is more sinister (the actual Latin word for 'left'). Although not the case with managers generally, right-brain thinking traits are more or less universal among the top leaders I met.

Intuition is a very familiar experience that permeates every aspect of business as well as personal and social life. Even those who are not particularly creative, or who cannot judge people intuitively, seem to have recognised the benefits of these 'skills', making up for any personal shortcoming in this respect in the choice of their team, frequently drawing also on the female intuition of their wives.

THE ROLE OF PERSONAL AND BUSINESS GOALS

As well as thinking in this bicameral way, leaders seem to know where they are going in both a personal and a business sense. They are quite happy with goals and objectives. But these form part of widely differing thinking styles, and motivate the leader in different ways. There is an interesting personality model that places goals in the categories of knowing, having or getting, doing, relating (to people) and being. These are termed 'life contents'. Each of these tendencies becomes apparent when we examine how different people achieve their personal or business goals. For example, some people are concerned with acquiring things (getting/having), while others want action – to have a go (doing). Some like to get as much information (knowing) as possible before they act, using knowledge as a form of power. In other cases relationships are uppermost, the consideration being what will *others* think, or do. But the *being* category is rather special, in that our desire to know, do, have or relate is usually towards the end of being – being financially secure, being comfortable, being respected, being happy, and so on. This fundamental desire to *be* is invariably central to any study of human excellence, and leadership is no exception.

Each of these life contents categories cropped up in the leaders I met. Some were concerned with outward evidence of their achievement, such as having a spacious office or the best car. Others stressed information (knowing) or getting involved actively (doing). But each of these tendencies was more of a personal route than a destination. Knowledge was for some *purpose* – like doing or getting. An activity (doing) was always with some further objective in mind, like having or being. Rather than just examining the life content of doing – based on observable behaviour – I tried to see the leaders as total persons, with a whole portfolio of life contents. (These life contents form a cycle, and usually follow a unique sequence for each individual. This is explained in *NLP: The New Art and Science of Getting What You Want*, [Piatkus]). This begins to reveal the essence of the person behind the behaviour.

YOUR PERSONAL THINKING STYLE

So how do these business leaders think? Thinking involves using the five senses inwardly – especially seeing, hearing and feeling – of which seeing images is the most common and powerful. A lot of the leaders I met are self-confessed 'visualisers' – they tend to see things mentally, before acting or making decisions. Others became aware of such a tendency as we talked. Keith Oates, MD of Marks & Spencer, will visualise a forthcoming meeting so realistically that the actual meeting, for him, is like a replay. He says, 'I now understand from my intense interest in sport [Keith is a member of the Sports Council of Great Britain] that this is a similar process for top sportspeople. They visualise scoring a goal or a point before the game in practice and in their minds.' As it happens, a far greater proportion of sportspeople than top business leaders are adopting successful mental techniques; the practice dates back many years.

Len Simmonds, who was then with T Bailey Forman, the Nottingham newspaper group, has similar experience, and a lot of what he does operationally can be an anticlimax, as the real 'fun' has already happened, in the form of vivid visualisation. John Hoerner, CE at Burtons, 'plays back' in great detail, and quickly, a visit to a store earlier in the day, then makes decisions or delegates action based on what he 'sees'. He then 'erases' the picture, which has done its job and is not replayed again.

Rodney East at Etam thinks particularly in pictures and colours. In an almost literal sense, he will see a warning red light or a 'go ahead' green light on some issue or decision, and this is his intuitive cue as to whether a course of action is right or wrong. He, along with others, will also use acronyms or mental structures to aid his thinking and memory, and ensure that ideas are not forgotten. Although we may each prefer to think in pictures, sounds (or words) or feelings, the ability to visualise in this way is just a natural skill, and is one that can be developed. Mental skills improve with practice, just like physical skills. It is a part of leadership that can be learned.

Being able to out-think others, be they colleagues, competitors or so-called experts, brings with it enormous personal influence, and is part of a leader's personal power. Indeed it is central to many of the leaders I met. Many were able to visualise several scenarios – often very quickly indeed – and thus test them out in a way that a non-visualising person is not able to do. A similar skill is employed when considering a candidate for a post. Interviewees are rapidly imagined in the various scenarios they might encounter, and matched with other employees and the culture of the company. This is something that no CV or psychometric test can match. On a bigger scale mental scenarios will foresee the results of a merger or demerger, product launch, or any other major change that a chief executive may have to deal with.

It appears to the impressed follower that the leader can quickly get to the core of a matter, is able to see the longer term implications, or somehow knows just what the important questions are. All of these often-quoted features of good leadership relate to an ability we all have, to visualise, that can be improved with practice. In people-decisions it comes over as sound judgement. Or a leader might be seen to remain cool in the heat of a crisis. In fact, for the leader, the crisis has already been 'experienced' in the form of visualisation – it comes as no surprise. For the leader, it is just another scenario that has turned into reality.

Synaesthetic thinking

Visualising is not the only form of inner 'experiencing'. A leader might exhibit auditory or kinaesthetic (feeling) thinking skills. But visualisation ranked high among the leaders I interviewed, helping in feats of memory as well as in imagining future scenarios. A developed use of all these thinking senses (or representation systems), known as 'synaesthesia', gave some leaders what seemed to be a particular advantage. For instance, a facility for remembering names (calling on auditory thinking powers) as well as faces (using mainly visual powers) can be used to great effect in creating rapport with people, as 'natural' salespeople well know. Auditory thinking usually means good listening skills. It is also related to internal dialogue, or self-talk. Lots of leaders were familiar with this inner thought process, which can be very motivating, sometimes taking the form of an inner guide or mentor. This again is a natural and universal mental process, as we criticise, encourage or prod ourselves. But it can be used in an empowering way that helps us to achieve our goals.

A far greater proportion of top leaders, as compared with the hundreds of middle managers I have trained, seem to have stumbled across this way of thinking. Add to these auditory skills a sensitivity to *feelings* – about people, information, business ventures, decisions – and the leader is equipped to face any problem he or she meets. Rapport with people is to do with matching thinking preference – a visualiser gets on well with a visualiser, 'feeling' people hit it off, and so on. So the synaesthetic person can relate well to all kinds of people. Neither person usually knows why, and puts it down to personal 'chemistry'. Personal thinking style – both the range of representation systems, and the extent to which these are developed – rather than intellect as we usually use the term, plays a big part in leadership.

Visualising for everyday success

Visualising is not a technique reserved just for high-level strategy, or for company issues. We use visionary skills all the time, and some people are more adept at this than others. A wife might be able to visualise just what the lounge will look like with a particular wallpaper, that suite she saw in a shop window, and some rearrangement of other furniture. The husband doesn't begin to appreciate how anybody can know what something will really be like without *actually* seeing it. Or vice versa. Some people just find it easy to mentally visualise things. Hardly surprisingly, this holistic right brain skill tends to result in better character judgement, and better people decisions.

It comes down to specific behaviour. Champion golfer Jack Nicklaus claims his best shots depend 10 per cent on his swing, 40 per cent on his set-up and stance, and 50 per cent on his mental picture, or vision. This confirms what has been called unconscious 'muscle memory', in which the whole physical operation simply matches the blueprint of the inner picture. John Hoerner, CE of the Burton group, locates files or specific documents by an ability to visualise the file and where a reference is – including exactly where on the page – as a mind-picture, rather than by following the logical filing system. There are many people who appear quite disorganised, yet use such a visualising skill with remarkable efficiency.

In each of these examples there is an instinctive and largely unconscious thinking skill at work – which, paradoxically, does not work when the conscious mind is brought into play. The intuitive right side of the brain takes the front seat in all sorts of feats of excellence – from a golf swing to choosing staff or meeting a company goal. This visual 'modality' is found everywhere where goals are consistently being achieved and personal excellence is evident. It is a big factor in leadership.

Thinking about how you think

Thinking style is revealed in other ways. Most quality thinkers are not aware of the *process* of their thought, in much the same way that great artists, musicians and sportspeople are not conscious of how they achieve what they do. Others, however, do think about thinking, so can throw some light on what gives them the edge. Bryan Castledine, chairman and CE at Erith plc, uses the analogy of a game of chess – thinking several moves ahead, testing out alternatives, knowing your objective, being confident that you can match any opposition, and so on. Ebbe Dinesen, CE of Carlsberg Tetley, is another chess thinker: 'Does it fit the strategy?' is his recurring question, as he visualises several moves ahead in the business. Sir Neil Shaw, executive chairman of Tate and Lyle, referring to their market penetration in Eastern Europe, talks of 'getting a seat at the table' – a poker analogy. David Varney, joint managing director at Shell UK, betraying a passion for Formula One racing, refers to the orderly state of the McLaren pit stop, the importance of the whole team, and the will to win, obviously drawing comparisons with business life. Metaphors and analogy are an important part of right brain thinking.

Rodney East, MD at the Etam fashion chain, uses the game of draughts as an analogy for how thinking can have its non-linear twists, remembering back to many games he played with his father in South Africa. Having made a move, and directing his own attention away from the part of the board in which his next show-stopping move would come, Rodney's tactic was to keep his finger on the piece for those vital extra seconds during which he might interpret his father's likely response. Out-thinking sometimes involves games within games, and the leader has to call on every part of his mental resources.

Jack Rowell, former CE of Golden Wonder and manager of the England rugby union team, can draw immediate analogies from different leadership situations inside and outside the business, not least the 'will to win', which is more a characteristic of US than British business. He sees attitude and personal motivation as far more important factors than DCFs (discounted cash flows) or systems and structures; his open, empowering, 'people' style – his whole way of thinking - reflects this.

Sir Anthony Cleaver, chairman of IBM UK, will draw as readily on cricket; Sir Richard Greenbury, chairman of Marks & Spencer, on tennis; David Varney on Grand Prix car racing; in too many cases to cite, golf provides the metaphors. John Collier, chairman of Nuclear Electric, makes a telling comparison between the necessary autonomy of his nuclear reactor managers and the captain of a destroyer, and in turn the admiral who determines the overall direction and strategy of the fleet. A good simile can make paradoxes and fuzzy situations clear. Leaders call on such simple analogies to maintain a sense of perspective, even in a large and complex business.

When the *process* of thinking is given conscious consideration - especially the intuitive part – we can sometimes surprise ourselves with just what we can accomplish. In most cases leaders stumble, in the course of experience, onto ways of better quality thinking. These ways of thinking are so unique and undocumented that much of leadership has become shrouded in the mystique of genetics or charisma, and seems beyond ordinary people. But the reality is very different. Ordinary people – you or I – can take on extraordinary leadership roles if we can learn to use natural thinking processes better than others. Every one of us can improve, with practice, our inner 'representation systems' – how we see, hear and feel inside; in fact, how we perceive. We are all able to have an *attitude*. We all know what it is to *believe* in something, and the power of such a belief. And we are free to have goals and dreams – including big ones. This is where real leadership is found. On the inside.

THE POWER OF INNER VISION

Vision has been a textbook trait of good leadership for generations. 'Without a vision', says the Old Testament, 'the people perish.' This wisdom, that long predates business schools, links in with our clearer understanding of the human mind and the nature of 'inner vision'. The role of visionary can make a manager a leader.

The visionary is more than a visualiser, although using the same mental skills. Vision involves visualising; but visualising may not produce vision – at least the sort of vision a leader needs to have. You can visualise the detail, but miss the big picture. You can see the trees, but fail to see the wood. Vision looks ahead, not just around. And the long-term direction of a company is firmly the responsibility of its leader, whose skill is in visualising – not just remembering faces, but creating a future, a dream, big enough and clear enough for others to follow.

Vision is very personal – it happens right inside. It is a word that was used little by the leaders I met – perhaps because of its grand, prophetic connotations. But the concept was familiar enough. The leaders talked about the future in plain terms: 'I get a very clear picture of what I want to happen.' They seemed to be able to *see* a situation – in some cases whole scenarios of the company or industry – in a way that was *real* to them, which could be described and communicated. What might appear in written form as long-term plans, or a proposal for a new product range, or a major acquisition, was turned – for the leader – into an unusual personal reality; a vision, dream or whatever. This personal vision seemed to account for the creativity, commitment, perseverance and sheer ingenuity that usually followed in its wake. Such a vision is likely to be infectious, creating the many followers who share it and make it real.

Regardless of the reluctance to use words with a prophetic or mystical connotation, vision is central to business and leadership. This is not to say that vision is found in all or even most companies - even though every company will have its share of natural visualisers - although it is talked about a lot. Nor does it sit comfortably with the logic, numbers and analysis that professional management is all about. But the concept is simple, and top leaders do not need to have it spelled out – it is an already instinctive part of how they think. By envisioning the future you want for yourself and your company, you are more likely to bring your goals to pass. Goal orientation has always been an important factor in personal and business success. The vision is what makes the goal a personal reality. Just like the work of an artist, your creation has to be real to you, and must come from the inside.

Following a dream

A strong vision guides, or perhaps drives, the leader in just about everything he or she does. It will inevitably give a leader the edge over the manager who tends to take a short term view of things, and who is motivated more by outside factors than an inner vision. As a thinking skill, envisioning gives the leader an advantage. The leader's dream – another word with its own connotations – gives direction and motivation, when others seem to be overwhelmed by events and circumstances.

Some of the leaders I met dream a lot – in some cases in the true daydreaming sense that we are all familiar with, but which we rarely admit to in work time. The practice seemed to be linked to a more general ability to 'see things clearly' both in terms of getting different perspectives on issues, and also in being able to take a longer-term view. Derek Williams, MD of Coca-Cola Schweppes Beverages (now CCSB) is a notable exponent of the art of daydreaming. Sir Keith Bright, until recently chairman of Brent Walker, also dreams a lot, adding that there is no point in imagining in a vacuum – creative thinking of this sort can be channelled into concrete company results. The daydreaming process is often the hotbed of the bigger visions upon which outstanding stories of corporate success are based, ideas that trigger operational improvements, or solutions to any kind of problem. But these people are far from being *dreamers*. Not many dreamers turn out to be leaders – or anything else worthwhile; but a leader has to have a *dream* – the distinction is important.

Ahead of your time

A vision can sometimes be hard to communicate, and initially it is unlikely to be supported by argument, analysis, or by the 'facts' of a situation. As a right brain creation, it may not be easily communicated in left brain terms of language and logic. It is a picture; but a picture, usually, of the finished article rather than a detailed plan of how to create it – a picture of the destination rather than the route. So the leader who seems to see beyond the horizons of his or her colleagues, or has a different perspective on things, can be frustrated. This is another feature of the leader that outward *doing* might not account for.

Sometimes a dream lies dormant. Sometimes it seems to be ahead of its time. Derek Williams at CCSB remarks that even after two or three years it can still be difficult to get a vision across, although the leader can instil confidence that he or she is going in the right direction – that is, confidence in the leader him- or herself. Sometimes it is enough to know your leader has a vision, that *somebody* knows where they are going. In other cases the vision has to wait its time, be clearly communicated, and subjected to all the rigours of rationale and analysis within the bureaucracy of the organisation.

Len Simmonds, former MD of T Bailey Forman, makes similar comments about having to deal with the frustration of others not seeing the potential of his ideas and plans. Or in the implementation process, with its usual pain and setbacks, he has to sustain motivation in those who might not yet see the reality of the accomplished goal. A specific business goal, perhaps for turnover in some part of the company, market share or profitability, may well seem unreasonable to just about everybody but the visionary – at least when the idea is first conceived and shared. The visionary leader has to live with these things.

BELIEVING THE VISION

Sir Keith Bright, former chairman of Brent Walker, had a 'dream' about growth in the Far East market that could not have been supported by any rational extrapolation of earlier performance, or equated with what competitors had achieved in a given timescale in that area. But his description of events contained a significant statement. As he put it: 'I began to believe it.' This *belief*, that accompanies a true vision as distinct from either wishful thinking or merely written plans, seems to be what correlates with eventual success. Belief grows as the vision becomes clearer. And the vision in turn becomes clearer. The picture inside takes on a clarity which is close to reality. For the visionary, it is *experienced* – so it has to be possible. It is believed, even though it is not yet known how it will be accomplished, or how the many obstacles in its path will be removed.

As we have seen, vision is personal – it should not be confused with corporate missions. Corporations don't have dreams or visions – people do. You can share a vision, but just with people. And nothing has greater power than an organisation whose people share the same grand vision. But it starts at the top, with the leader. As leader, you are not just an executive, the super-implementer of a thousand disparate visions from throughout the organisation, even though your personal vision might have grown from the seed of someone else's idea. Rather, you are the guardian of your organisation's vision and its culture. Others will no doubt excel in 'running with the vision' and seeing things through to a successful outcome. But this is not where a leader's priorities lie. By then you will be viewing more new horizons. Your role is clear. You need to have good mental vision. You have the power, as leader, to bring to birth your ideas. You have created something from nothing in the past, and that's why you can be a leader today.

Capturing minds with a big vision

A big vision – underwritten by personal commitment and belief – can capture minds and imaginations more easily than a set of numbers or a well-researched business proposal. Robert Lawson, CE of Electrocomponents, talks about setting 'unattainable goals' for his people. Like Sir Keith Bright, he was assuming in his goal-setting a level of compound growth that had not been achieved in the past. So new parameters had to be set. The status quo had to be questioned at every turn. But he was staggered at the way his people captured the vision. Once the vision is taken on board, 'left brain' critics can become allies, and show just how the goal can be made attainable. With new assumptions and perspectives, supporting figures can illustrate the whole thing is feasible. The goal becomes *owned*, and the commitment of a lot of people translates the dream into reality. In the case of Electrocomponents a whole new strategy emerged, involving acquisition as well as internal growth. But instead of being a sterile strategy or business plan with no personal champion (with which businesses are replete) it was the natural outcome of a captivating, impossible dream.

Interestingly, an earlier and somewhat more ambitious goal had backfired, leaving a negative impression on the people. But in my interviews I probed what I think is the crucial difference between a published mission statement or corporate plan and a true vision. In the more recent, highly successful case, Robert could '*see* it happening' – however logically unattainable the goal seemed, even to him at first. He *believed*. And that belief, rather than the absolute money value of the target (£1.5 billion, as it happened), was the critical factor in success. The slogans and emblazoned T-shirts of the earlier goal could not match what was achieved by personal belief and vision.

Roger Burnell, MD of Britannia Airways, defines vision simply as the ability to see ahead. But he adds that it is 85 per cent to do with people. The vision is what produces the personal energy and all the spin-off traits like commitment and perseverance upon which the leader's success depends. But the leader's success lies in others. Corporate success demands a shared vision. So, once experienced, the leader's vision has to be translated first into a shared vision, then into achievement on the part of all the people involved – sales, quality, and business growth. But, always, the bottom line numbers follow the vision.

Standard brain hardware

Vision belongs with the soft, mystical side of management and sits uncomfortably with the doing, macho part of a modern manager's armoury. It is to do with how we think; how we use the mind, and specifically the natural visualising skill we all have to some extent. For this reason vision rarely appears in a management job description, although it suddenly becomes a key issue when you reach the number one position. Vision concerns not the analytical side of our thinking, but that part that is concerned with imagination, intuition and creativity. Its raw material is images, rather than words, numbers and abstractions. Not being verbally articulate, the mute right brain cannot even express a good case for the things that it does far better than its left brain partner. Hence its bad press, and the dominance of left brain thought processes, glorifying formal logic, verbal reasoning, analysis, and western IQ testing.

Fortunately we have learned a lot from neuro-physiology about these different modes of thought, carried out in the two sides of the brain. In calling on visionary powers, the leader becomes a right brain thinker – able to imagine scenarios that as yet do not exist, able to make mental pictures of otherwise abstract goals. In a quite literal sense, he is able to experience *subjectively* (seeing, hearing and feeling inwardly) something before it has become reality *objectively*. So you can start creating your own vision using standard brain hardware and software; a vision for your personal future, your department, or profit centre. That's leadership thinking.

I've been here before

In my discussions with chief executives, vision was strongly linked with creativity, insight, perspective, and other characteristics we associate with effective leadership. Leadership is about becoming more aware of your own inner processes; adopting a new style of thinking and perceiving; learning to see yourself and your problems in a new way. The way the thinking process is described is most revealing. In some cases the vision of a goal is so real that the reality, as Len Simmonds describes it, is an anticlimax. There is the feeling, 'I've been here before.' The real 'activity', for the visionary, is in the visualising. Even intricate or minor obstacles can be foreseen and 'handled' at this stage. The euphoria of a goal achieved against all the odds might then be left to the implementing staff, as the leader's buzz was in the idea, perhaps a eureka, or in the confidence of a clear mental vision. So a visionary leader might soon get bored with the operational side of the business. To such a leader a problem is solved when it is solved in the mind – a goal is as good as reached when it can be clearly envisioned.

All this is anathema to the logical left brain thinker, who needs to see with the eye rather than the mind, and to handle outwardly rather than feel inwardly. But it is a mental tool the sceptical, analytical thinker could do well to cultivate. The visionary thinker uses mental skills as much to test ideas as to form goals. Nine ideas might have to be abandoned before one becomes a corporate plan, but the elimination process will have been based on far more than pros and cons lists, or strengths and weaknesses analyses, or consultancy exercises. It will have been based on the power of the imagination to bring together a myriad variables to represent a future scenario far more accurately than any spreadsheet or system. Using the lounge example, if a dozen mixes of wallpaper and furniture can be pre-visualised, it saves the expense and effort of actually creating each possibility. Because all the inner senses are invoked in this natural process of mental rehearsal, the chosen scenario will *feel* as well as look right. And this feeling of 'rightness', when it comes to pondering the future and major decisions, is something the leader comes to value highly. It comes from clarity of inner vision.

How do these right brain thought processes stack up against the 'planning, control, evaluation and monitoring' of the professional manager? They come into their own when judgement rather than a logical answer to a black and white issue is called for. When data are missing or inadequate, when assumptions have to be called into question, when people's opinions and attitudes form part of the situation – in short, in the real world of uncertainty and change. They serve you well when time is of the essence.

You can visualise several scenarios very quickly, whilst holding a conversation or doing something else, and so get a 'feel' for a situation that might otherwise have taken days of fact finding and analysis. And even then, the 'evidence' of a logical process of investigation might be so finely balanced in its pros and cons that subjective judgement is still needed for the final decision. These intuitive powers come into their own when you are evaluating quality rather than measuring quantity, or when people are the main consideration – such as in choosing staff or conducting a sensitive negotiation. And they are indispensable when you are interested in creating the future rather than analysing the past – that's what vision is all about.

The creative mind can create something from nothing – it doesn't have to rework what has gone before. So in a constantly changing environment where nothing seems predictable from past experience it becomes the leader's ace card. The innovators in business are not the MBA analysts, but the right brain visualisers. The best leaders excel at both kinds of thinking.

Communicating the vision

What is inside the leader has to come out. To start with he has to share his vision, communicating it in such a way that it will turn it into reality. This can be a problem for even the most distinguished corporate leader. Some rely upon one or more board colleagues to interpret their feelings and back them with any argument and logic needed, thinking through the implementation implications and tying up the loose ends. So there is a 'bridge' to left brain colleagues – perhaps the finance director – who do not speak the language of feelings and vision.

There is immense value in the sobering influence of a logical thinker at this top team level. As one chief put it about a colleague, 'He *is* my left brain'. In other cases the chairman or CE was as analytically minded and articulate as his peers, and could readily communicate his vision, influencing the very culture of the organisation. So the leader with strong visionary traits either knows how to choose and lead a balanced team and so communicate to the organisation, or enjoys the less common bicameral brain characteristics of an Einstein – the formidable partnership of cool logic and verbal skills, and boundless imagination.

The central theme of this chapter is that a leader's power lies inside. As a leader, before you have a following, you have to know yourself – your strengths and weaknesses, dreams, values and beliefs. Many leaders find themselves 'by accident'; others date their clear vision a long way back. The great psychologist Carl Jung expressed something similar:

Within each of us there is another we do not know. He speaks to us in dreams and tells us how differently he sees us from how we see ourselves. When we find ourselves in an insolubly difficult situation, this stranger in us can sometimes show us a light which is more suited than anything else to change our attitude fundamentally; namely, just that attitude that led us into the difficult situation.

We might not all use the 'royal road' of dreams, but we can all call upon right brain, creative, intuitive powers; powers that sometimes seem to come from another source – yet which we know are born inside. This is the sixth sense of the leader. The sooner you stop trying, and tap into your inner resources, the sooner you will know what it feels like to be a leader.

TIPS FOR TOMORROW'S LEADERS

1. List some of the activities you need to be more confident about, which you associate with leaders. Grab opportunities to practise any of these, if necessary manoeuvring your way into situations. Be prepared for some mistakes. Picture yourself excelling in these situations, whilst daydreaming or before going to sleep at night.

2. Think about how you think. Do you get frequent flashes of inspiration? Do you have to *feel* right about decisions? Or does everything have to stack up logically? This self-awareness is an important start to tapping your leadership skills.

3. Determine your 'life contents'. You can easily put your goals into the categories (knowing, doing, getting/having, relating, being) by the words you use: 'I'd like to *have*', 'I'd like to *be*', etc. You can also change their relative importance. This is the inner you, and you can always change what's inside.

4. Think further about how you think. Do you like to think in pictures – visually – or are you an auditory (hearing) or kinaesthetic (feeling) sort of person? Do you, for example, find it easier to remember people's faces than their names? Start using inner senses you are not so familiar with when exploring memories and anticipating forthcoming events.

5. Start developing an inner vision about where you want to be, what you want to do. Repeat and clarify your inner vision until it becomes very real. Check that it does not conflict with other goals you have, and amend your desires so that there is harmony in different parts of your life. See yourself as a leader, and get to know also how it sounds and feels. Be a leader at home as well as at work – you are changing who you are, not just your job role.

6. Start using your thinking powers in everyday situations. When hiring staff, imagine them in the different roles they will have to play. If reorganising an office system, visualise clearly what things will eventually look like. Incorporate these thinking skills into every part of your life and work.

7. Practise also long term visioning – perhaps a dream holiday or a couple of jobs ahead, or retirement. This is a learned skill, not a leadership trade secret.

$$\boxed{3}$$

The Intuitive Leader

WE ARE ALL CREATIVE, all of the time. Every sentence you speak is a creative act. You express your creativity in everything you do, every decision you make – whether resolving a conflict, organising a presentation, or preparing a meal. We need plenty of ideas to do well in any field, together with sound judgement, and insight, and imagination. A leader needs to have a good flow of ideas to stay abreast of the business, the industry, the customer, and a changing world. Quality ideas are rarely the result of logical, left brain thinking. We might logically reach interesting conclusions, as computers do, without getting what we call ideas. Ideas, or insights, tend to come intuitively, often as surprises, sometimes as 'bolts from the blue'. Whatever they are, and wherever they come from, the leader learns to recognise and harness them. According to Derek Williams, MD of Coca-Cola Schweppes Beverages (now CCSB), leaders are 'logically obliged to be intuitive, by the very nature of their function'. In this chapter we shall see the importance of intuition, ideas, and some of the characteristics of this sort of thinking, with examples from the leaders' own experience.

NO BLUEPRINT FOR THE FUTURE

The past has less and less relevance to the changing future – there is not much that is sequential or logical about real life and business. Consequently, however many years' experience you may have, the fact is that you have no reliable blueprint for tomorrow, let alone two or three years ahead, which is where any textbook will tell you the CEO should concentrate.

As well as cold analysis, the leader needs judgement:

- about people – staff, customers, suppliers, bankers, investors – and how they will behave

- about how and when technology might impact the business and in what timescale

- about changes in the world around them that affect the business.

More than anything, the leader has to bring creative thought to bear – fresh ideas – in seemingly ordinary situations.

Many middle level managers, sadly, are quite unaware of their blinkered vision. They hide behind logic, analysis and verbal reasoning – it is possible to become almost addicted to rationality, even justifying failure in plausible terms. In turn, there can be cynicism about any creativity we, and others, might naturally display. But the comfort of rationale will not suffice in today's business. The information revolution means that even the smallest companies have access to extensive market intelligence and the latest technological innovations. More and more, the playing field is levelling.

The leader's special value to a firm is that sense of perspective, originality of thinking, some hard-to-define skill that sees more than the 'facts'. You have to be able to spot significant connections between data that are quite unrelated, filling in the gaps when data are missing or riddled with unsupported assumptions, or are not relevant to the real issue. You need the courage and self-confidence to question logic and analysis, and the opinion of experts. You have to avoid getting swamped with detail, yet know when detail is needed. And the buck stops with you; you have to make the hard decisions. More than that, you need a whole way of thinking that can be translated into committed followers and corporate success.

Not every idea we get is earth-shattering – most never see the light of day. Even Edisons and da Vincis see only a tiny percentage of their ideas coming to fruition. So we need plenty of ideas. Having said that, at the level of the CEO, with a perspective of the whole company, a good idea is as likely as not to be of some strategic importance. Even a single good idea can result in a change of direction, new products and markets, an acquisition, or big profits. As Michael Wemms, retail director at Tesco puts it, 'Plant a good idea and it will grow'. The aspiring leader has to recognise and harness even a whisper of an intuition, and give crazy ideas a fair hearing.

BUILDING ON THE IDEAS OF OTHERS

Ideas don't have to be new ones. Even the most creative leaders do not claim much originality. Mike Jackson, CE of Birmingham Midshires Building Society, credits the highly innovative First Direct bank with some of the ideas he has used in a major transformation of his building society. Jack Rowell, former CE of Golden Wonder, refers to 'fast followers'. He is not too proud to borrow ideas from the US 'Chicken Tonight' company and other leading players in the snacks business, and adds that a lot of ideas come from the packaging specialists in the industry with their close customer contact. Richard Gooding, CE of London Luton Airport, says 'Don't start out to be number one.' He draws ideas from other airports, as well as from comparable businesses in the UK and abroad, such as shopping malls. Indeed, few of the leaders I met claimed any great originality of thought. Stanley Kalms, chairman of Dixons refers to himself as a 'mongrel innovator', with the confession, common amongst top leaders: 'I've never had an original thought in my life.' Archie Norman, chairman of Asda, is an 'assiduous copier.'

All this, I think, was more than false modesty on the part of these leaders. It reflects the fact that ideas draw on what already exists, both in the world around us and in our individual experience. It is the *association* of disparate bits of information that produces the new neural connections that we call an idea. The secret is in knowing who to follow, and spotting links with your own industry and situation that may not be obvious. There is no system or conventional training course that can ensure that you make these associations. The harder you try to be creative, the less it seems to happen. But you can start with knowing that your brain hardware is as good as the next person's. We all get good ideas from time to time. Start expecting more from your intuitive right brain.

RECORDING YOUR IDEAS BEFORE THEY ARE LOST

Ideas have an ephemeral quality – they can be there one moment, and gone the next, replaced by another line of thought, and perhaps emerge later in a different context. Because thoughts can be so transient, one of the secrets of quality thinking is to be always ready for ideas when they come, and to be open enough to allow them to develop and expand.

It was interesting to find, in this high tech age, that the most popular and often quite indispensable management aid is a little notepad measuring about three inches by four, on which ideas are scribbled down before they are forgotten. Although these notepads were packaged differently, from fancy leather-bound little wallets with personally overprinted stationary to loose paper offcuts, their function was the same – to capture those fleeting ideas from the creative brain. They are the only recording system used widely when having a long, hot, creative bath (several dictaphone recording machines have been ruined during such creative bathing). 'One scribbled word is enough', says Peter Smith of Marconi. Even some of the joggers among the leaders I met are known to use this management tool when out running. In fact some of these leaders were notebook addicts, and would suffer from some form of phobia if they found themselves in a restaurant or having to wait for a while without their notepad and pen. Usually the habit originated after brilliant ideas were lost because they were not immediately recorded. Such recording systems say more about the value of spontaneous ideas than the organising skills of the leaders.

Although some people have no difficulty in recalling ideas that come just before going off to sleep or in the middle of the night, night-time revelations can be especially problematic if you are not to disturb the whole household. In some cases mental tricks have been developed to ensure a brainwave can be recollected the following day. Sir Nicholas Goodison, chairmen of TSB, dates his creativity back a long way. When at boarding school he would record ideas he got during the night on the white wall next to his bed, which acted as an ideal writing medium in the low light. Today, like so many others, he insists on having a white wall close at hand, in the form of a little notepad. Others just trust their memory, and insist that few good ideas are entirely lost. Andrew Lloyd Webber, the composer, is familiar with creative times as tunes come to him. He manages to get away with not recording everything at the time it comes to him and his philosophy is simple: 'If it's good I'll remember it; if it's not, it doesn't matter.'

This 'trust' in the memory is another aspect of a well-used right brain, and some leaders could do quite well without pencil and paper, or dictaphone recorders. Ideas might come 'the day after the night before' when showering or shaving in the morning, or some time during the day, usually triggered by a sight or sound, event or conversation. The main thing is to understand how and when these transient ideas come, and to find ways to remember them.

STAYING READY FOR IDEAS

Of course we need to be mentally open to ideas whenever they come, not just in the small hours of the morning or when travelling – which can be in the turmoil of day-to-day life. Rodney East, MD at Etam, tells of an occasion when he lost his car keys in Milton Keynes. Spending the long wait for the AA in a McDonald's restaurant, he devoured every bit of literature and advertising poster in the place, watching closely the whole operation. As a direct result of this he came up with ideas for a 'crew bonus' for his staff, and a self-tuition training programme with suitable awards and recognition – all since successfully introduced at Etams.

The long journey home, high up in the front of a large AA

breakdown vehicle with a panoramic windscreen, was a new experience – a film director's view of everything as they drove along – and an idea was born relating to their own store windows. Traditionally a store front was the side windows divided by the necessary entrance in the middle. The result was that neither side was wide enough to house an impressive panoramic presentation such as he experienced from the AA van, particularly if, as was often the case, the store front was narrow to start with. So a forthcoming store development was planned with the door to one side, leaving the maximum window display width, which could be used far more effectively. And the ideas did not stop there. He later spotted a competitor's store with a very *high* window presentation, and this too was exploited in a Scottish store which was long and narrow, but which had plenty of height. Thus the impression of a great mall, or film set, was achieved, turning a 'problem' into a winning idea that made the awkward-shaped property stand out from all the local stores.

Any circumstance – including a negative one like lost car keys – can be turned round to give positive results if the mind is receptive. Creativity is not a question of having a thinking slot programmed into your crowded time manager system, although that might well help. It is a habit – a natural receptiveness to new thinking. And the smallest of ideas can develop into important business changes that would not have resulted from any known analytical technique. And one idea often leads to another, and another. You just have to stay mentally open and expectant.

Getting more ideas than you can handle

Idea generation is a common leadership factor, and several of the CEOs I met were particularly articulate about this all-pervading way of thinking. Keith Oates at Marks & Spencer 'never stops' thinking up ideas, and asking questions.

'There are always more ideas than you can handle', he says. 'It is important never to be satisfied, always to search for improvement, for new products and better methods.' Vernon Sankey at Reckitt and Colman makes the same confession: 'I never stop thinking'. Ideas can come to him at any time, anywhere. Robert Wilson of RTZ talks about two ideas a day. I recall that Stanley Kalms, chairman of Dixons, gets closer to six. The managers at London Luton Airport have come to expect to hear from Richard Gooding, their CE, on his almost daily walkabout: 'I've had an idea.' Len Simmonds, former MD of T Bailey Forman, always comes back from a tour of the site with three or four ideas. Don Bennett at Texaco used to be known as 'Data Don' – thinking all the time; to Don everything is a puzzle waiting to be solved. Martin Laing, chairman of the Laing construction group, is another idea- (or more)-a-day man who sees everything as a problem – a stimulating challenge. In volume mode the quality of ideas varies a lot, and not many get through the test of a leader's own left brain, let alone the rigours of the company's appraisal systems. But, as Keith Oates points out, 'there are always plenty more ideas.' With these people, productive thinking has become a habit, so without conscious mental struggle a constant supply of ideas is assured.

Such creativity is by no means unique to leaders. On the contrary, it is widespread, but in the case of most employees it is usually seen outside of the work context, perhaps in the form of a hobby or pastime. The leader channels this creativity into personal and business goals, and everyday decision-making.

The flow of creative ideas

The experience of creative thinking is as unique as it is fascinating. John Sunderland, who heads the worldwide confectionary business of Cadbury Schweppes, uses the metaphor of pieces of a jigsaw coming together: this applies particularly to decisions about people. The colleague of one leader says 'a bubble starts to form over his head, and I know an idea is coming'. Tom Vyner at Sainsbury's talks about an idea 'rolling around' in his mind. Ideas-people get a lot of pleasure from this part of the thinking process, which is not confined to the business, but is more a way of life.

The 'flowing' phenomenon is not unique to business leaders. On the contrary, managers generally have been slow to tap into their creativity. They tend to be 'left brain dominant'. Most professionals have had their childhood imagination trained out of them by their professional bodies, or conditioned out of them by their mainly bureaucratic organisations. Scientists, artists and writers for many years have said a lot about a flow of creative thought that seems to come from an outside source. It is so common that the remarks of Enid Blyton, the children's writer, although extraordinary, are merely typical:

First of all, you must realise that when I begin a completely new book with new characters, I have no idea at all what the characters will be, where the story will happen, or what adventures or events will occur . . . I shut my eyes for a few minutes . . . I make my mind blank and wait . . . and then, as clearly as I would see real children, my characters stand before me in my mind's eye. I see them in detail – hair, eyes, feet, clothes, expression – and I always know their Christian names but never their surnames (I get these out of the telephone book afterwards). . .

Sometimes a character makes a joke, a really funny one, that makes me laugh as I type it on my paper – and I think, 'Well, I couldn't have thought of that myself in a hundred years'! And then think, 'Well, who did think of it then?'

William Thackeray wrote something very similar about the 'observations' of one of his characters, asking: 'How the dickens did he come to think of that?'

But this is the very process that intuitive leaders speak of. Referring to one idea that came to him 'out of the blue', Rodney East, MD at Etam, remarked: 'I could never have thought up that solution in a million years.' That is the quality of intuitive thought – ideas emerging from the subconscious right side of the brain. I heard Rodney East's comment repeated again and again as I got to know how these leaders think and make decisions – what gives them the special edge.

Creative thoughts can have an almost physical pressure – 'I can feel them forming; then everything "flows",' says John Sunderland. The flowing analogy came up again and again. A major report or speech might almost 'write itself', and this after weeks or months of barren attempts, or mental impasse. A system or organisational structure idea might come complete and in minute detail. John Sunderland notes particularly the high quality of what comes out of these special thinking experiences. A report, for example, would probably not need rewriting. An insight can have immediate relevance to the job. A spell of hot weather raised an intuitive red light in John's mind about the sales of chocolate and other confectionery, which traditionally suffered during hot weather. Although the figures and reassurances should have quelled his fears, his gut feeling had to be checked out, and, sure enough, it turned out that the short-term forecasts had been over-optimistic, for the very sensible reason he had predicted.

RELYING ON GUT FEELINGS

Derek Williams of CCSB defines intuition as 'An unconscious anticipation mechanism.' Or, as one CEO put it:

'Intuition is our door to the future': it can address the future rather than the past. The main benefit of a 'gut feeling' is that it comes a lot quicker than logical thought (which is usually used to rationalise after the event), so there may just be the chance of doing something about the matter – such as bringing expenditure into line with falling revenue before net profits disappear.

When developed as a thinking skill, gut feelings tend to be right more often than not. They do not depend, it seems, on what happened in the past. Nor are they filtered by political or organisational distortions. Although drawn from a person's 'hard disk' of past experience, it is the *association* of many apparently random things from the past that makes special sense. It is the very *absence* of political factors, and so-called received wisdom, that makes many instinctive ideas seem far-fetched. Only with hindsight can the true value of these insights be measured. At the time it takes trust and courage to follow them. And that is part of being a leader. True intuition, rising from the subconscious, can produce the very best first time round. It can even sort out priorities, and rank the issues to be addressed by the subconscious mind. Sir Neil Shaw, executive chairman of Tate and Lyle, speaks of 'intuitive priority rating' and instinctively ranks his markets, for example, so that effort and resources are properly channelled.

The leadership secret is in recognising signals from the subconscious – real intuition rather than prejudice or wishful thinking – trusting these, and having the courage to act on them before their potential value has gone, notwithstanding the cold logic of your own left brain and wise colleagues. Warren Bennis listed courage among the attributes of a leader. We are now beginning to see where courage is needed – in being true to your gut feelings even when you are out on a limb.

Succeeding without trying

Sometimes thinking is a very conscious process. You *know* you are thinking – usually about a specific problem – and you can almost feel the cogs in your brain turning around. This conscious, mainly left brain thought has been given most attention in our study of the brain and the human mind, in the form of logical or sequential reasoning. This is where we make the association with computer programs. Then there is the easier, more freewheeling sort of mental wandering typically carried out on a long car journey, or on a railway train, or when having a bath or doing some relaxing work such as gardening.

Derek Drake, MD of Servowarm, finds his one-and-a-half hour drive to work an invaluable time for such free thinking. During those times all sorts of thoughts might flit through his mind, as issues are sorted out, internally debated, and given some priority rating. On other occasions a single pressing issue might fill the whole of the travelling or other free time, but again the matter in hand will be viewed from many different angles, as possible scenarios are visualised. Occasionally a eureka might slip into one of these sessions, something not linked to the several topics of freewheeling thought, and this is one of the pleasures of quality thinking. The paradox is that you don't work hard for these brilliant ideas or solutions to problems. You don't *try* – at least not with this kind of thinking. That is why a lot of hard-working managers never become real leaders.

'Not trying' is another feature of creative thinking that keeps occurring. This was the essence of what Timothy Gallwey found when he pioneered the new coaching techniques for top tennis players that he describes in his book *The Inner Game of Tennis*. He identified two 'selfs': self 1 was the critical self that *thought* he knew all the answers and was always ready to criticise and offer advice; self 2 was the inarticulate self that just got on with playing the game, and had all the natural, childlike skill. And the two were always in conflict. When left to get on with the game, self 2 would be at his best, enjoying himself and not conscious of what he was doing. The injunctions from his other self to try harder, or correct this or that, only made him perform worse. The analogy is, of course, close to our present understanding of the way the left (self 1) and right (self 2) sides of the brain operate. And the secret is always, in all sorts of activities involving skills or natural talent, to 'stop trying.' This is a bit much for the macho left brain manager to swallow. But the enlightened leader knows that there are occasions when it is sound advice.

Good questions

More often than not, ideas come in the form of *questions*. And a good question can get you well on the way towards an answer. These questions can form a sort of inner dialogue, or 'self-talk', again during a long drive or when you are not likely to be interrupted. Questioning can also be evident in interpersonal situations such as when we 'bounce' ideas off others.

Rodney East of Etam talks of discussing an issue 'Socratically'. Andrew Michel, former MD of FKI Babcock, when exploring a subject, finds himself asking strings of questions of a colleague, as his way of probing creatively some problem or issue. Interestingly – and this is so typical of the way intuitive thought operates outside our normal consciousness – he often does not know *why* he is asking a particular question – the questions just come out. 'Why did I ask that?' is what goes through the conscious mind afterward. Only with hindsight will he realise just how insightful the questions were, even though not consciously formed. Robert Ayling, CE of British

Airways, also uses this form of intuitive questioning to clarify, or get to the core of an issue. The human mind seems to move relentlessly towards understanding and meaning – it has got to have an answer. The right brain in particular, with its holistic view of any situation, is a most sophisticated tool for this questioning process. Suppressed, or silenced by left brain rationale, it can become a tragic waste of the ultimate human resource. Even half an idea might be enough to form an insightful question. And a good question will stimulate more ideas.

It is not uncommon to link an ability to ask probing questions with good leadership. But it does not follow, from all our research, that such questions follow a pattern of formal logic. A well-prepared manager has probably gone over the issues logically before ever a report or proposal reaches the boss. What comes across as surprising, perhaps show-stopping questions, are the non-logical ones – the lateral, insightful ones that express a feeling rather than known facts. 'How on earth did he come up with that? He has only just seen the proposal', is the common sort of response. This is the intuitive, right brain at work, and it gives a leader the special edge.

Going against the trend

The best ideas often have a strange tendency to go counter to popular trends and received wisdom. Bryan Castledine at Erith opened up a new region during the depths of recession on the basis of his intuition. With hindsight, as is usual in his experience, it made sense. Logic tells you that every recession comes to an end eventually, and that it makes sense to make structural and other changes at times of low activity when sales output is not sacrificed, or even that another region might be subject to a different timescale in the boom and bust profile, or that other regional factors have to be considered. But at the time, gut feelings that go against the tide – in this case of the whole industry – need brave leadership and self-confidence.

The thing that marks out these ideas, and the people who get them, is that they stray a long way from the obvious, and often elude the experts. Only with hindsight do good ideas become common sense, and so obvious with hindsight that the originator is usually denied any credit. David Varney described a logistics problem that Shell UK had, concerning the delivery of petroleum by road tankers to North Sea ferry terminals. The solution was to deliver by barge in the harbour. The barge acted as a warehouse and overcame the problems of tight ferry schedules, allowing the elimination of road deliveries. That was a single idea that brought big marketing and environmental benefits.

Nuclear Electric made massive savings by changing the incentive system that applied to the annual mainteance shutdown of plants. Not uniquely, the overtime system they had historically applied resulted in a longer rather than shorter period of shutdown, with all the costs involved – that is, it had the reverse effect to what was intended. Once the problem became clear, plenty of creative thinking followed, and recurring savings of millions of pounds were achieved. The winning idea, however, flew in the face of all the entrenched attitudes.

Len Simmonds, formerly at T Bailey Forman, makes the point that the ideas of leaders can be ahead of their time. This is always the danger when, by nature, you are concerned with the future rather than the past, and your vision often goes ahead of your people. So you need to be able to deal with the frustration of others not seeing the potential. Not only might your staff not see things as you do, equally the customer might not. Even when an idea is introduced, often the groundwork is painful, and it needs a clear vision and belief to keep going. Len Simmonds, for example, because of his involvement with the education sector, was aware many years ago of how commercial and competitive education would become. His difficulty was that it was a lone view at the time. Nevertheless, his job was to keep the thing alive. Today, education editorial and advertising features are big in the minds of his Nottingham Evening Post readers, and significant for the company's revenue.

The best ideas people come up with concern *what might be*, rather than what *is* – they can look into the future. In particular, they do not accept the status quo. Everything is subject to change. The leader is constantly questioning what we are, the way we do things, and the way others do it. Some leaders make very good non-executive directors because they are able to question on a broad front, seeing beyond the detail. Leaders are restless, they have to live with the frustration of sometimes seeing horizons that their managers cannot see – creative solutions that are beyond other people's imagination.

There are specific creativity techniques that stimulate ideas in this way. One technique called 'reversals' reverses any true statements about a problem or the company, doing in effect a 180 degree turn, to explore the issues that the reversal throws up. Some of the successful leaders, it seemed, were just using such techniques, or other unique mental devices of their own, that had the effect of breaking out of entrenched mindsets.

The blindingly obvious

Most good ideas, it turns out, have been staring you in the face all the time. Rodney East was stuck with a long-term lease for accommodation well beyond Etam requirements, which threatened profitability. From any angle it was a problem – all the classical 'logical' solutions such as subletting had been considered and thrown out. On a management walkabout, and completely out of the blue, an idea emerged that would mean full profitable use of the building. 'Traditionally Etam, besides normal fashionwear retailing, had undertaken 'cut, make and trim' (CMT) operations, which were central to their intended strategy of increasing self-made garments. Although potentially profitable, hitherto CMT had been just a small part of the business, done by subcontracted labour. The idea was to bring this operation in-house in the available, spacious accommodation without the usual incremental costs, at the same time increasing the scale of CMT operations as part of an already agreed strategy. In this case a 'problem' – coupled with not a little fear as to the financial outcome of the underutilisation – opened up a major strategic opportunity. Theoretically the connection could have been made at any time; in reality, because of the long tradition of subcontracting and the previous low weighting of CMT in the business, logical thinking and analysis did not do the trick – day-to-day business gets all your attention. The change came from an intuition – an idea thrown up from somewhere below the subconscious.

This case illustrates well the need for some goal or problem for the mind to work on – it doesn't operate in a vacuum. In this case Rodney's unconscious mind brought together an agreed but somewhat optimistic strategic intention to grow a certain part of the business with the more present problem of rental payments. The solution, as ever, was blindingly obvious. On later reflection, however, he could not envisage an analytical process that would have brought about such an outcome – however obvious it was with hindsight. Fortunately, he had learned not to depend on logical solutions. We need to be open to these mental gifts if we are not to miss the obvious.

First impressions

Sometimes intuition and gut feelings are associated with first impressions. They can come very quickly – say when initially presented with a problem, or on meeting a person for the first itme. Robert Solberg took over the European Texaco upstream operation at a time when it showed up in a poor light in terms of market share, output, and other key indicators. But one bit of the data, connected with the level of unexploited North Sea oil deposits, did not seem to fit the dismal pattern of the rest of the facts. On the strength of an intuitive feeling about the importance of that one single factor, Solberg began to view the whole situation from an entirely different, and more positive angle. At the same time he marshalled key people who were able to see beyond the 'logic' of an overriding negative situation. The result was a fundamental strategic change of direction for Texaco UK, with internal structure and systems to match, and a remarkable turnaround of the business. Trusting that hardly definable inner voice, that 'just knows' something is right, or wrong, or significant, is part of the courage that keeps appearing as a top leadership trait.

In this case Robert Solberg had the strongest impression of how the European operations should go when he was relatively new to that part of the business. It was what we call a first, or an early impression – at odds with the years of hands-on experience many of his colleagues boasted. But first impressions, as regards both people and also the essence or core issues of a business, can be important examples of intuitive thinking. Sometimes a fresh mind is needed.

In his very early days as MD at Berol, the pen manufacture, Jonathan Bowman identified what he saw as the major issues that had to be tackled. The actual changes implemented over the following months – after all the necessary checking out and communication – turned out to be not just very close to his first intuitive impression, but right for the company. So there is a *quality* of thinking at play, that takes an holistic view of a situation, and turns out to be clearer than a more 'correct', rational and lengthy process.

With hindsight, of course, we often wonder why we did not trust our first impressions. There is an evolving 'intuitive maturity' on the part of leaders, in which they learn through experience to trust their judgement. And this compares with a known tendency for more junior managers to be biased towards dominant (left) brain thinking, when roles are more prescribed and decisions are based more upon systems. Most leaders confessed to being more intuitive today than they were ten or fifteen years ago. Some had become increasingly sceptical about techniques and systems. The demands of top leadership seemed to call on 'softer' thinking skills, in which initial impressions play a part.

On joining Irvin (GB), the market leaders in parachutes, Mark Warland went through a similar initial period of assimilating the key issues in the business, some of which were of strategic importance and required fast decisions that did not allow for a period of back-pedalling. In this case, in order to get an edge on the competition for a forthcoming tender, Warland's intuitive decision was to design a parachute from scratch – a major, complex venture. Although critical to the future of the business, this was counter to the rationale as expressed by those who patently 'knew better', and involved a timescale close to impossible. Once again, however, the intuitive judgement and decision turned out to be the right one. This illustrates the importance of courage and personal confidence on the part of the leader, as well as of recognition and trust of early impressions.

Eurekas

Sometimes ideas really do seem to come out of the blue. These are the memorable ones which can be so

extraordinary, both in the way they come and in their significance to the business. Sir Richard Sykes at Glaxo will never
forget one idea that came to him while riding his lawn
mower in New Jersey – a complete solution to a problem,
after literally months of thinking. Roger Burnell, London
Luton Airport chief, was also mowing the lawn when a solution came. This related to the replacement of a retiring
director, and other important organisational changes that
would coincide, although there was nothing unique about
the nature of the problem, with its usual mixture of people
and politics. Some very 'sensible' proposals had already
been discussed with his top team, but Roger 'did not feel
comfortable' about them. When the solution came, everything was so clear, and it seemed that the answer almost
came from an outside source. Moreover, with hindsight, it
was a patently more 'logical' solution than the one he had
felt uncomfortable about.

In both these cases the issues had been simmering below
the conscious level for a long time. In the latter case Roger
had actually given himself a personal deadline to come to a
decision, which was neatly met by the weekend in question.
Interestingly, although the right brain will usually not be
constrained by conscious deadlines ('I want a flash of inspiration by five o'clock, please'), it does seem possible to 'pro-
gram' a deadline into the subconscious, much in the way
that some people can wake up each morning at a predeter-
mined time. Derek Williams, at CCSB, ranks this high
when he says 'the mind has to have a deadline.'

Sir David Alliance, chairman of Coats Viyella, cites a
memorable eureka. He was watching the film *Lawrence of
Arabia* when the answer to a problem he had been grappling
with for a year hit him like a thunderbolt. It was to do with a
computer application and complex programming that had
defeated the big company experts. 'I've got it', he shouted,
much to the surprise of his friends and fellow cinema-goers.

Not much sleep followed for Sir David and the startled executive with whom he shared the revelation by telephone.

Brian Maguire, MD of Golden West Foods (the main suppliers to McDonald's) was travelling on a train when the solution to a complicated problem concerned with the 'flour ferment system' came to him. Bryan Drake at Servowarm got a 'brilliant' idea when lost in the music and staring blankly at a spotlight at Chichester Festival theatre.

It seems highly improbable, from the descriptions I got, that these insights would have resulted from any logical, conscious process of thought. They were too good. One CE was convinced that even a succession of brainstorming sessions would be unlikely to match the quality of a real eureka.

Ideas, whether they evolve over a long period or come as eurekas, don't happen in a vacuum. They fit into some current or latent problem or issue, even if this is not at a conscious level. And the leader is rarely in a dilemma about what do with intuitive ideas. Each eureka actually solved a problem, met a need, removed some barrier, and took the leader and his company closer to some goal. Leadership is not just about getting ideas, but about getting good, useable ideas. A good leader can turn a fleeting intuition into hard business results.

COMMUNICATING YOUR IDEAS

A common problem an 'ideas person' has is in *communicating* an idea – maybe a grand vision, or perhaps just some subtle feeling – to others. The right brain, of course, where creativity largely stems from, does not handle language well. The logical left brain 'scores' almost every time, winning arguments and forcing decisions on rational grounds what-ever the comparative quality of the ideas. So the really cre-ative person seems to be on another plane – 'he lives in another world,' as we might say.

A leader often has the same problem, especially when his ideas disturb the status quo, or happen to be a little ahead of their time. But he can only achieve anything tangible through people. He is hopeless on his own. So he has to be able to communicate well, and this indeed is a feature of good leaders. Accordingly he is unlikely to be a right brain thinker only – like an artist, creative designer, or inventor. He is just as likely to have a highly develped analytical brain. A paradox perhaps – at the same time imaginative and intu-itive, and yet also rational, analytical and articulate. He is *bicameral* – using both sides of the brain. A leader's mental resources are stretched in two, often conflicting, directions. Facts and feelings, heart and mind, intuition and logic – they all have to be reconciled. If you have ever been 'in two minds' about anything, you will be familiar with the experience. But this brain balance is what quality thinking is about.

The same story appears among scientists and other noted thinkers. Many had to toil with their 'two minds'. Roger Sperry, the Nobel prizewinner in physiology, propounded convincingly the 'two mind theory.' His research showed that, quite literally, we have *two* minds in the form of the two brain hemispheres.

This is what Francis Galton, the British inventor and pio-neer of the science of fingerprints, wrote as a four year old.

My dear Adele,

I am four years old and I can read any English book, I can say all the Latin substantives and adjectives and active verbs, besides 52 lines of Latin poetry. I can cast up any sum in

*addition and can multiply by 2, 3, 4, 5, 6, 7, 8, 10. I can
also say the pence table. I read French a little and I know the
clock.*

Francis Galton, February 15, 1827.

But as Galton wrote later in his life:

*It is a serious drawback to me in writing, and still more in
explaining myself, that I do not so easily think in words as
otherwise. It often happens that after being hard at work, and
having arrived at results that are perfectly clear and satisfac-
tory to myself, when I try to express them in language I feel
that I must begin by putting myself on quite another intellec-
tual plane . . . after I have made a mental step, the appropriate word frequently follows as an echo; as a rule, it does not
accompany it.*

It is unlikely that Galton would have made it as a captain of
industry. His communication skills would have let him
down. Few of today's business leaders reveal the extremes of
creativity of the great scientists or writers. Where these have
combined both language and 'cerebral' skills and inventive
excellence, we class them as geniuses. But where a person
simply uses both sides of his brain a bit more than average –
or *both minds* – we begin to see special results. And in this
category belong many of our leaders.

So the mystique is gone. These people have simply –
somehow – kept the imagination, curiosity, and creativity
we all had as children, but which in most managers and
professionals has atrophied with non-use, just as an arm
or leg would. But also, usually through education and professional training, they are as happy with logic and verbal
reasoning as the next person. So they know and use their
intuitive sixth sense, yet can communicate their dream and

feelings – relating to people through the mind as well as the heart. This combination is what gives the leader, for instance, judgement in choosing people, and the intuition needed for finely balanced decisions. This is the source of 'people power'. Intuitive leaders can express themselves well and get what they want from others. They have their feet on the ground. They are as happy dreaming up some crazy idea as carefully masterminding the implementation of a dream. And they are using natural thinking abilities that every one of us have, and that we can improve with practice.

TIPS FOR TOMORROW'S LEADERS

1. Be ready to borrow other people's ideas. It happens in the best and highest of circles.

2. As a rule, go for volume in ideas. One winning idea will make up for all the ones you have to discard. And the practice is good for your overall creativity.

3. Find a system to record your ideas whenever and wherever they come to you. A little notepad might be all that you need – but don't leave home without it.

4. Learn to recognise and trust the subtlest of instincts when they do come. Check them out, of course, and watch out for prejudice and wishful thinking. But don't discard ideas just because they are wild or because they came from nowhere. Give them a chance.

5. Be ready to receive ideas at any time, for example if you are delayed when travelling. Expect to come out of annoying or negative situations with some good idea to show for it –

some positive outcome. Stay open to your thoughts in the most unlikely of circumstances.

6. Be ready to think and act against the trend. Don't be different for the sake of being different, but when strong feelings and intuition demand such.

7. Have respect for first impressions – about people, places, or any new situation. You don't have to act immediately on these, but register them in your conscious mind and record them. They will probably turn out to be of use.

8. Think back to any 'eurekas' you have experienced. Then try to recreate the circumstances – if need be, adjusting your lifestyle – so that you start getting more of them.

Creating Solutions and Making Decisions

MANAGEMENT is all about solving problems – the best business leader is a problem solver *par excellence*. Any goal or objective can be treated in problem-solving terms – you are at A and your problem is you want to be at B. The problem might be a minor operational one, or it might be of strategic or even vital significance. In the case of top leaders, it might concern the choice of a fellow board member, a critical client negotiation, or opening up a new market or product range. The ability to address problems holistically, rather than just in a classical, analytical way, is a characteristic of top leaders. This chapter looks at the thinking processes leaders use to solve problems and make decisions. The intuition and ideas in the previous chapter form a part of this.

THINKING ABOUT PROBLEMS

There are different stages in the process of solving problems or making decisions. Whilst few top leaders follow any conscious model of thinking – or for that matter, style of behaviour – they do seem to recognise and use each of the stages that have been identified with the problem-solving process.

This book is thin on theories and models, but the well known stages set out below do place some of the less understood ways of thinking into a simple pattern. See if you recognise these in your own experience.

Preparation

This is the stage at which we gather data, analyse the task, state the problem, and make and question assumptions. It is associated with the planning stage of a task or project, such as a building, or a wedding. It is also linked with the goal-setting that is usually associated with good leaders. If the stage is missed out, goals tend to be missing or unclear. Although it has usually been linked with left brain thinking, the most common missing element in this stage is usually the ability to see a goal clearly, in the form of visualisation. It is this right brain function which can bring a sterile plan to life. It is what produces the vision we have already discussed. And the same sort of skill is used to restate a problem, see it from different angles, question assumptions instinctively as well as logically, and so on. Sir John Hoskyns, chairman of the Burton group, talks of 'walking slowly round a problem'. You cannot invest too much time in this stage. Big things are born. Direction is determined. The future begins here. The true leader is no shoot-from-the-hip manager, but a statesman who thinks ahead.

This is not a very active time for the manager who wants to get on with things. It involves more thinking than doing. There may therefore be the tendency to write lists, construct charts, or do *anything* that avoids the passive job of thinking. With practice, visual preparation – or mental rehearsal – can create the buzz and emotion of the real thing. But vivid imagery of a future scenario can include things that will not work, and that feel wrong, as well as the ideal end result. So a lot of pain and expense can be avoided. Solutions can be *tested* mentally.

Frustration

This stage involves feeling bored, irritated or despondent when you cannot resolve an issue. Honest managers will readily admit to this happening. We know what it is to get stuck. There is a feeling of discomfort, perhaps inadequacy. There may be doubts as to whether any solution exists at all. For all these reasons we like to skip the stage, jumping ahead to get on with a less than adequate solution, or just do *anything*. It requires patience, but this is a vital stage to go through. Targeted towards a clear goal, frustration urges the unconscious to work and eventually produce the insights and flashes of inspiration that will make the waiting worthwhile.

This stage is frowned upon by educationalists and bureaucratic bosses. It is seen as a sign of muddy thinking or indecision. We are culturally conditioned to see frustration as symbolic of weakness, or even failure. Were Beethoven or Michelangelo never frustrated? Did they not experience blocks in their creativity and output? Did Newton's ideas always flow smoothly? Van Gogh describes how frustration was a major part of his life, and Einstein lived with it for years. This is part of problem-solving, and an indispensable part of leadership. We have to trust our own creative process. Frustration is a signal to stop trying too hard. Think about something else, or do something completely different. It requires, usually, a change of attitude. If you can hold onto this state for a while without getting too negative, the 'creative tension' can sometimes help you break through to another level of thinking – perhaps seeing the problem in a new way. There is no known technique to overcome frustration – so don't do anything. Sleep on it.

Incubation

This is the next stage. It is a time when you give up trying, put the matter on hold, and hand it over to your unconscious mind. Like incubating an egg, it seems all we are doing is keeping an idea warm – on the back burner, if you like. In practice you *do* need to do something – something completely different. We might enter this stage voluntarily, saying, in effect, 'I want to sleep on this problem.' Or it might overtake us by default, as we declare, 'I give up. I can't go any further.' Or we might be sucked into another matter that assumes priority. The stage can last for minutes, such as when we break for a coffee or go for a short walk, or it can last for weeks or months. Like frustration, this part of the problem-solving process is not given the status it deserves. It simply does not square with the image of a modern, positive, active, decisive manager.

But many creative people are very familiar with this phenomenon and carefully build it into their work and lives. The novelist Graham Greene, for example, having completed all his research, and gathered all the facts, experiences and impressions he needed, did not immediately sit down to write. Instead he would wait, allowing his unconscious mind to take over, and would watch what it had to tell him *in his dreams*. Only when his dreams had gathered and settled did he begin to write. But don't worry if you don't remember *your* dreams. As we have already seen, ideas reach our consciousness in many ways. Seymour Cray, founder of Cray Computers, has a different approach. For many years he has divided his time between building the fastest computers in the world and digging a tunnel that starts beneath his house. 'When I get stumped, and I'm not making progress, I quit. I go and work in the tunnel. It takes me an hour or so to dig four inches.' For Cray this is more than a simple diversion.

Says the chairman of the company: 'The real work happens when he is in the tunnel.'

Incubation can be unintentional. We take our mind off a problem for a moment, perhaps during a meal, and the answer suddenly pops up. Most answers to questions can wait for 24 hours – if not, for at least ten minutes while we have a break and think about something else. If you squeeze insights out because of your crazy deadlines – which were probably the result of poor planning in the first place – don't expect quality answers. If you want to be a leader, you have got to become familiar with this stage.

Insight

This is the inspiration – the 'aha' moment that we often associate with creativity. It is the memorable part, and featured much in the accounts of the leaders I met and their stories in the last chapter. But if insight is all there is to the process, we are quite helpless, as we are usually little more than spectators, or willing beneficiaries of what comes from somewhere below our consciousness. The creative leader, however, knows that although insight seems to have come from nowhere, it actually occurs as a result of everything that has gone before, including the mental struggling and frustration, and the incubation. The insight usually comes when we are doing something quite unconnected with the problem and are in a relaxed state. The new idea, intuition, insight, or however we describe it, may be triggered by something totally unconnected. The following instance is typical, and illustrates some of the features of this stage.

A senior information systems manager was walking past the Natural History Museum in London when the word 'Savannah' came to him. The word soon became a very clear image, and its meaning developed – but it all took just a few seconds. He remembered how, when he was twelve years old, he had visited one of the first nuclear-powered ships with his father. On a lower deck, the guide had opened a hatch and through a plexiglass door they had looked down into the engine room, and saw the mysterious, thundering engine. Now, 24 years later, this memory of the ship *Savannah* spoke to the manager and triggered a new realisation: he didn't have to know all about himself to go forward. 'The captain of the *Savannah* didn't understand all about the atomic reaction inside his ship. But still, he could navigate it on a foggy night in unknown waters.' This was the 'message'.

This is typical of many insights, in that it did not relate to a known problem, or at least one that could be easily described – although the 'solution' was of unmistakable benefit. It was also highly personal, so that the incident might have little meaning if told to someone else. The significance comes also with the strength of feeling that accompanies the insight, the clarity of the visual image, the surprise at the long-forgotten memory, and the relevance to some very present issue in your life. The high speed compares with the chemistry of first impressions we saw in the last chapter. The associations involved may be so tenuous that we cannot consciously understand them – in this case, perhaps, the association between the museum and the word 'Savannah'. It is the synthesis, rather than the disparate memories, that make the 'sense'. So in the case of personal chemistry, for instance, we may simply not know just why we like one person, and dislike another without any reason.

Sometimes the insight is an image rather than a word or words. Einstein was lying on a grassy hillside, looking up at the sun through half-closed eyelids, imagining himself to be a light beam travelling from the sun to his eye, when his inspiration about the nature of light occurred. But that was after years of preparation, frustration, and incubation.

Techniques such as brainstorming, lateral thinking, and

synectics are closely related to this stage. But while these techniques might stimulate ideas, they do not really address creativity, which might well depend upon the amount of groundwork that has gone on, including all the frustration, as well as the important period of incubation. They are techniques, not solutions. Solutions lie inside, although they often seem to come from outside (because of the operation of our two, distinct minds, the right brain being largely unconscious in its operation). We usually say 'it occurred *to* me'. The key, therefore, is not in techniques, although there are good techniques which apply to some of the stages, but a receptive state of mind, and respect for the process. Self-trust is a big part of it. So-called creative people are not creative because they have more ideas, but because they trust them, and are willing to explore them. That's why I stressed at the start that leadership starts inside the leader.

Working out

This final stage involves checking out the insights and putting them into some form. An artist, writer, or business leader has to work hard to make their ideas become reality. In business, creativity must be transformed into innovation, and eventual hard results. This is the pragmatic stage, when concrete steps for implementation are planned and executed. Of course you will need plenty of creativity to face the practical problems involved in this stage, but each of these are separate problems which will follow the same process I have outlined. The cycle starts over again.

This stage also requires communication skills – ideas have to go *outside* the creative leader, so it is usually associated with the verbal, communicating left brain. But here again, the perceptive manager will think of creative, effective ways to get his message across. Feelings as well as facts may have to be communicated. The testing part of this stage might mean going back to the drawing board, as Thomas Edison did repeatedly, and the process starts over again.

GETTING TO KNOW HOW YOU THINK

Most leaders are familiar with these stages, seeing them as different *ways* of thinking. They can often be identified with different kinds of problem, different times of the day, different places, or different moods. Each kind of thinking plays an important part in the total process. Deliberately, consciously addressing an issue firmly registers it for further unconscious processing. Making time and personal 'space' for freewheeling thought, during which the mind can wander without a fixed agenda, choosing its own priorities and concerns, allows different memories and awarenesses to surface, enabling the mind to make those clever associations of otherwise insignificant facts which seem to be at the heart of creative thinking. John Conlan, CE at First Leisure 'prefer[s] not to talk' at these times, describing his way of thinking as completely 'unstructured'. Although personal experience differs, being ready to accept and trust a thought 'presented' by the subconscious mind is part of this holistic way of thinking. Top business leaders seem to have got to know something about how they think personally, and they build on what the mind does so well if given the right freedom and stimulation.

The problem-solving dance

Aspects of the thinking process I have outlined, which has endless variants, were described hundreds of times in the discussions I had with top business leaders. Without being aware of, or concerned about, any overall process of thought, these leaders were quite familiar with each stage, and the order in which they occur – particularly the significance of 'sleeping on a problem'.

There do, however, seem to be short-cuts. For example, a ready-made solution might hit you during the preparation stage. That's fine. But consistent, creative problem-solving does not rely on short-cuts, but follows a habitual way of thinking that uses both sides of the brain – the conscious side and the unconscious side. What the process really shows is a dance between these two sides; intuitive and logical, unconscious and conscious. Both sides are involved in each stage, but take on different roles, choreographed according to some purpose or goal. The secret is in two-sided – bicameral – thinking.

IDEAS TRIGGERED BY PROBLEMS AND NEEDS

The ideas we discussed in the last chapter that mainly form the insight stage don't appear in a vacuum. However vague or unconnected, they usually relate to some problem, goal or issue, even if it is somewhere below the conscious level. A current problem or issue, whether consciously understood and articulated, or just 'felt', seems to 'call for help' from the mind's subterranean resources. In the same way, the mind is strangely focused when there is a measure of fear – if we know the bailiffs are coming round on Friday, we will probably do some fast and very creative thinking. Or if a key customer is threatening to switch to a competitor, all sorts of mental ingenuity is triggered in the company.

Jerry Swan, MD of Caterpillar, came up with some of his best ideas during a period when the company was in 'survival mode'. As he put it: 'Desperation sometimes leads to brilliance'. Mark Warland, MD of Irvin (GB), says 'ideas are triggered by need.' And Archie Norman, chairman of Asda, says he does his best thinking in a crisis. David Watkins, MD of Lucas Hartridge, doesn't mind large, intractable problems. When others are swamped, he rises above and looks down on a problem, knowing there is always an answer. This is so typical of top leaders – some seeming to thrive on problems. The holistic, or helicopter view, the belief that there is an answer, the confidence in yourself – all these kept cropping up in our discussions.

Ideas address whatever is a problem or issue to the individual at any time. So the chairman's ideas will tend to address the chairman's problems. A junior manager's ideas will tend to be more operational or functional. And ideas will relate to business or non-business issues, to the extent that either is dominant. For the leader, they will tend to reflect what is then uppermost in his or her personal and business priorities.

The problem or issue itself is the fertile ground in which the mind does what it does. Sir Nicholas Goodison, chairman of TSB, remarks that his creative ideas tend to fit with the bank's well-formed strategy. Given a clear overall purpose or goal, intuitive thinking will tend to move in the direction of those desires and goals – even unarticulated ones – however lateral and innovative the ideas might have to be to achieve them. Robert Wilson, CE of RTZ, says 'If you don't have a strategy, anything goes.' So a clear vision, rather than the vacuum of not knowing where you want to be, is the fertile environment for insight and surprising, intuitive thought. Whilst needing little help in providing ideas about how to get there, the right brain wants to know where you want to be. Although not needing much help in solving the trickiest problem, the intuitive part of your brain likes to know what the problem is.

Goal-directed ideas

The problem or issue becomes the goal to which the mind is directed like a missile aimed at its target. Goal-orientation is, of course, a feature not just of leadership, but of achievers of all kinds. But the vision, or visualised goal, sometimes mystically associated with a leader is the very environment, or purpose, in which the intuitive mind flourishes – it does not respond to a written corporate plan. The stronger the goal, the more the unconscious mind will be harnessed to offer solutions at every step of the way. The clear goal illuminates insights which would otherwise remain hidden. Stating the problem clearly – say in writing – usually gets you a long way towards its solution, even though the nature of the real problem might change. But the leader adds another dimension in being able to visualise, or mentally rehearse, the desired outcome. He *creates* the solution inside. This is the thinking power that gives him the edge – he can see the solution. (Techniques for setting and clarifying goals, and visualisation techniques, are included in my earlier book on neuro-linguistic programming.)

You can't separate the leader, and his ideas, from the business. As Derek Willams, MD of CCSB, puts it, he is a 'walking agenda'. The leader, he says, operates within a 'circle of lifespace', and never goes outside it. His lifespace includes what is important to him, and at the top level usually the business is overriding. And his ideas, intuitions and feelings will all reflect this lifespace. A bigger circle will result in more ideas, which reflect the leader's needs, desires or purposes.

DECISIONS UNDER PRESSURE

Frequent and often courageous decisions are required of leaders. Such decisions are an occupational hazard for some, although relished by others. They are needed particularly at times of crisis, or even of survival, and mark out the real leader from the regular manager. Robert Solberg at Texaco spent a period working with the group president which turned out to be one of the most demanding periods of his life. The company was then going through the worst experience in its long history – facing bankruptcy and other litigation on a scale unique even to the industry – and every day was filled with great unknowns, major decisions, and deadlines. Life generally, and business in particular, was all about surviving until bedtime. But during this period he learned much about the uncanny powers of intuition in the absence – sometimes the complete absence – of supporting data. As assistant to the group chief, and a relatively junior executive, he was able to help steer the business through its toughest time. He did not have the years of experience then to match many of his colleagues, but even forty years of experience can be rendered close to useless when a business is operating in uncharted waters. Not only are real leaders able to call on intuitive powers that equip them for such challenges, but often they relish the experience, which becomes as routine as writing up a sales ledger.

SLEEPING ON THE PROBLEM

The incubation period we looked at earlier is where many managers get it wrong. They do not have the patience, and are unable to associate conscientious management with any form of inactivity. Simply by accepting the need for this stage, a manager can take on an important leadership characteristic. Sir Keith Bright, formerly chairman of Brent Walker and also of Electrocomponents plc, tells of an important idea to do with tidal energy (which is a particular interest of his), which came to him as a memorable 'eureka' after more than a year of deliberating on the problem. A sort of compulsory incubation (literally 'lying down', from the Latin) of thoughts also happens during sleep. The following morning often brings a welcome new perspective and fresh ideas. Top leaders have learned that you often need to sleep on a problem. It is not very macho, and contrary to modern, analytical management methods, but quality results demand these thinking resources.

One Friday morning, Graham Cooper, then MD of Autotype International (part of Norcros), knew instinctively, and certainly, that an important decision he had been toiling over about a top US appointment was the right one. Although the implementation of the decision would not be easy, mentally he had turned an important corner. Like the other leaders I spoke with, he did not really understand how it was that simply 'sleeping on the problem' could so change his outlook.

Based as they are on the wider lifetime store of data below our conscious level, decisions reached in this way tend to be more dependable than conscious, grinding, analytical thought. As a leader, you will require a lot of trust in your intuition, and a good measure of self-confidence, if you are to overcome the battalions of left brain rational thinkers determined to justify their self-fulfilling arguments. But it will serve you well. It is surely a clever leadership trick to turn 'lying down' into a time management and problem-solving device.

STRATEGIC THINKING

Sometimes the problem is not a specific, operational one, but one that concerns the whole company and its future. Maybe the problem as such has not even been defined, and the leader needs to get some direction, vision, or perspective on the matter. The best leaders seem to have an uncanny ability to simplify things to their lowest, common sense level, at which they are easily and convincingly communicated. They get a 'big picture' perspective on issues. The comments I got from directly reporting senior managers were 'He gets it right so many times', or 'You have got to do your homework before you go in.'

This clarity about the essence of a problem, the markets, or the business, is what makes the difference at strategic level, and separates out those with muddy thinking. And it is more than corporate planning. I met few fans of precise planning processes. For top leaders, planning was more linked to personal vision. It was the big picture – graphically clear, in that it could be described in just a few words or with simple metaphors, although usually based on an intricate knowledge of the business. Key issues were always being sought – taking care of those key issues is what business success is all about.

Along with this is the confidence and positive attitude – and this is surely a top leadership trait – that *any* problem can be solved. But choosing between the important issues and the 'line noise' is not something that can be trained for in a logical way. Many highly intelligent, rational people make silly, short-sighted decisions, and poor people judgements, frequently devoting all their attention to minutiae. At the highest level a sort of sixth sense is more likely to come into play. As Robert Wilson at RTZ puts it: 'Issues don't come out and hit you.' Such thinking is frequently described as coming 'from outside' – lateral thinking, if you wish. But you cannot abrogate your own thinking responsibility, nor delegate it to even the most competent manager, as you might an organisational change or profit responsibility. Such thinking surely has its place at every level in the business, not just in overall direction and strategy. So for corporate success, the creative leader has to be an example, a model, rather than the fount of all ideas. Out-thinking the competition might just mean having the basic sense and skill to think like a customer rather than a manager, or 'putting yourself in their shoes' – seeing things from another perspective.

Strategic thinking put into practice

While at Golden Wonder, Jack Rowell talked more of 'filling technology' than about snacks, or potato crisps, the apparent product of the company. So, for him, venturing into pot noodles did not represent a departure from the core business ('from packs to pots'), although the synergy of the opportunity might well have been lost due to blinkered vision. Mike Jackson at Birmingham Midshires sees his building society clearly as a retail business – shops. Peter Ellwood has the same marketing view of the TSB bank. This sort of approach not only makes clear what you are, but how you do things – your whole attitude to the market. Every retailer then becomes a potential model, every high street a potential source of valuable ideas.

Retailing analogies, including one-stop shopping, are now fashionable in the marketing departments of the high street banks. But decades of 'customer first' have not entirely removed the entrenched cultures that are still a long way from the 'happy shopper' ideal. Clear thinking is demanded, starting with the leader, and this does not come from analysis alone. On the contrary, too much analysis is more likely to cloud the vision, or focus on the wrong issues. There is much to be said for a strategy that 'feels' right, and involves heart as well as mind, or, more accurately, both sides of the brain. These are the characteristics of clear focused thinking that seemed to mark out the exceptional leaders.

The introduction of the Marks & Spencer chargecard,

and later a whole range of financial services, was a departure for the company at the time, and an important strategic move. Keith Oates, who joined as finance director, master-minded what has turned out to be a very profitable part of the business. But it involved a philosophy which was new to the company, which, as a retailer, was geared to turnover and short term profitability, rather than longer term returns. So the change was hard to swallow – 'You won't make a profit for three years.' Questions, for example, about whether to enter the then buoyant home mortgage business required a fundamental re-examination of the company's strengths and image in the market place. Repossessing poor mortgagors' houses might damage the firm's well-earned image of excellence and customer care. The instinctive deci-sion, as it happened, was against entering the mortgage business, but to do so for some other financial services. The own-chargecard decision, just as important, and just as dependent on the intuitive feeling of 'being right', turned out to be a good one. As the leader, you must think strategi-cally; but any idea might turn out to be important for the very future of the business. As a problem-solver and ideas person you are an example, a role model, setting the climate for a creative, people-based culture.

Understanding your business

However it comes about, the 'right brain' thinking we looked at in the last chapter is sometimes needed to get a clear view of the business, and how you relate to the market place and competition. This is particularly the case when an issue is complex, or is full of unknown factors, or, at the other extreme, is so familiar that you need to see things with a fresh perspective. And creative thinking can apply as readily to internal systems and structures as to market and product strategy.

Irene Graham, MD at Target Life, used part of one weekend to come up with a flow of ideas which resulted in an important restructuring of the company. In this case, organising according to process rather than the usual product or region (the fund had been 'closed' so the usual marketing rationale did not apply) allowed significant efficiencies and cost savings to be achieved – besides being common sense. In these cases the ideas came easily – 'they just seemed to flow' – although the subject had been given plenty of conscious thought. Difficult problems need not require difficult solutions. Insights – as distinct from long-thought-out conclusions – are often devalued because they seem so simple and obvious. They can also come as a *surprise* – that is, there is an element of 'eureka', even though with hindsight the solutions are common sense. As Lilian Bennett at Manpower describes them, they are GBOs, 'glimpses of the blindingly obvious'.

An idea might not be as well packaged and complete as some of these examples. It might be more of a perception, a clearer understanding about the nature of the business and its market, or about a personnel issue, or just another angle on a problem. It might address, for example, what business you are in, or want to be in, rather than your strategy, how you plan to get somewhere.

Leslie Hill, now at Central TV, had a major problem while chairman of a group of glass companies (itself part of a larger group). One company specialised in making walls for squash courts. He recognised that they were not really in the glass business at all, but rather the squash rackets business. As a result of this he decided it did not fit in with the rest of the glass business, and proceeded to dispose of it. This proved difficult since it was very much a one-off kind of company. It was in the early days of management buy-outs, and it occurred to him that this would be appropriate for an MBO. The company was successfully disposed of in this way, and in turn has been successful outside a diversified group. Now and again such insights follow from a SWOT (strengths, weaknesses, opportunities, threats) analysis, or a special research project. But at this fundamental level, intuition rather than any systematic approach is usually the stimulant for a whole new perspective. It often takes lateral or intuitive thinking to decide that a glass manufacturing company is not in the glass business. The link with MBOs – a big factor in the solution – illustrates how creativity is about associations; thought links, where otherwise irrelevant ideas make for synergy in a bigger, winning idea.

Competitive solutions

'Heart' thinking is needed in all sorts of situations. From time to time, for example, you need to discern whether a person can be trusted or not. You might call this intuition or a 'gut feeling', but, whatever it is, you don't get far in dealing with people without it. Similarly, beating the competition on price or delivery might mean abandoning cherished, once adequate practices, turning conventions on their head, and this rarely happens using logical problem-solving techniques. Indeed, if ideas are always generated through some understandable, linear process, a leader is hardly needed at all – there are plenty of inexperienced but numerate and analytical managers, and even computer programs that can reliably carry out a series of logical steps. Such functions the leader can indeed delegate. More to the point, any competitor worth his salt will have read the same books or reports and be thinking along the same lines. So logical thinking is not the sort that creates competitive advantage.

Bob Lawson, CE of Electrocomponents, stresses the importance of intuition as a 'differentiator' in modern business. Competitive advantage is constantly being eroded by universally accessible information, from many sources. Systems, he argues, cannot differentiate, and we can no longer depend on analysis alone – they (the competitors) all have the same tools. Intuitive thinking breaks out of linear, me-too thinking. Bob Lawson echoes many top leaders in stressing the need for intuition and brain-power – referring to *whole* brain power. And this applies from the highest strategic level to the shop floor. He stresses that this is not resident in any one individual, although the CEO is an enabler within the company, creating both the example and the culture for the essential creative processes. The non-linear, for all practical purposes limitless right brain is the innate resource that provides the edge. This is the added value of leadership, and a key to competitive advantage.

SOLVING OPERATIONAL PROBLEMS

Ideas about day-to-day operational matters can be as fascinating as major strategic insights. Mark Warland of Irvin (GB), the parachutes company, was previously involved in the packaging business, and relates an innovation to do with sticking labels on bottles. The problem was always that the labels, when stacked, tended to stick together, making them difficult to handle, and seemed to defy automation. Then he noticed how workers on the line would dextrously bang the end of the stack of labels loudly on the table before fanning them, and completing the manual process with ease. By designing a machine to do just that – banging then fanning – the process was for the first time automated, with all the consequent benefits. Of course this was just common sense, which is what any good idea is with hindsight. This idea did not come while the boss was confined to the executive suite – he had to see, hear and feel the operation for himself, before his brain clicked. Nor had he to dwell on the complexities of such operations (the expert's considered opinion, or what is impossible), but the simple belief that there is a way (what is possible). Such possibility thinking is part of a successful leader's mental armoury, effective on problems whether they are strategic or operational.

Bob Hawley, CE of Nuclear Electric, recalls facing a more sticky problem than sticky labels. This concerned a component which needed to be covered with transposed strands (coiled wire in opposing directions), but the process, unfortunately, was protected by a patent. A study of the patent details revealed that the protected process involved ten opposing, wound strands of wire. When the intuitive answer came it was as though there had been no problem in the first place – use *nine* wires, or eleven – the exact number did not matter. However obvious the solution appeared with hindsight, the problem had seemed, to the experts, to be intractable. Rather than reinventing the proverbial wheel, at great expense, a little creative thinking was all that was needed.

David Lyon, CE of Bowater, solved an endemic problem concerning concrete gas flue roof fittings, which were prone to breakage in transport and handling. The ingenious solution drew from the technology of packing television sets with expanded polystyrene, and technology relating to bra straps developed by Courtaulds Textiles. As ever, the solution came from outside the industry boundaries, and did not arise from long-standing conscious thought, but from a lateral leap of the imagination.

Operational ideas, besides involving memorable creativity, can be significant in money terms, or have longer term spin-off value. Don Bennett had to convince his Texaco US top management about a radical approach to risk

management on a massive North Sea oil exploration investment. The success of his approach, which, although untried
and complex, was potentially worth millions of pounds, was
likely to hinge on his ability to communicate it to the parent
company mandarins. He then happened to see a virtual
imaging video in the course of his work, and knew immediately that he had found the answer. Virtual imaging technology and the video medium allowed him to get across, in
eight and a half minutes, the crucial message, and the new
policy went ahead with great success. In this and many
other cases a single unsolicited idea can translate into big
profits, and in some cases long-term strategic changes for
the better.

Leaders are not usually associated with super-creativity,
in the way that an advertising executive or design consultant
might be. This is largely because of their balanced, feet-on-
the-ground attitude that checks things out before implementation. But when real examples of creative thinking do
arise, they show not just the difference between a creative
leader and a more blinkered manager counterpart, but
the enormous potential for corporations when staff
generally are encouraged to think for themselves. Creative
thinking need not be 'bought in'. Given the right leader and
cultural environment, every member of the staff can make
a contribution.

Great comebacks

Andrew Freeman, managing director of hosiery manufacturers Atkins of Hinckley, left me buzzing with excitement
after our interview. Images of 1970s platform shoes, a
sporty steering wheel and a boomerang would not get out of
my mind as I drove home. The problem started for Atkins
when, because of a change of supplier policy, the big retailer
BHS delisted them as a main supplier. Working with a sales

promotional colleague who worked for no fee, the solution they came up with was unusual in the extreme.

A handful of key BHS executives were targeted. Somehow they had to be persuaded to change their minds about their policy decision. One Monday morning, the first director on the list received a package containing a sports-type car steering wheel, along with a little printed card headed 'Great Comebacks No.1'. It told the story of Niki Lauda's amazing comeback to motor racing: 'Niki Lauda will always be remembered for his triumphant return to motor racing after a horrific accident at the German Grand Prix in 1976 . . .' and so on. No mention was made of Atkins at all. Mike France, the recipient of the steering wheel, thought little of it, but the next morning he received another parcel, this time containing a pair of platform shoes and a card headed Great Comebacks No. 2, celebrating the revival of platforms in contemporary fashion. Day three brought a jockey's cap and the story of Bob Champion, who beat cancer to win the Grand National in 1981. By this time France had mentioned the parcels to one of his director colleagues who – surprise surprise – had also received the same deliveries. So had the then chief executive and the two hosiery buyers. By this time they were all intrigued, and awaited with anticipation Thursday's delivery. This was a compact disc and the usual little card, this time celebrating the comeback of the legendary Swedish pop group Abba. Still no mention of the sender, though.

They were all ready on the Friday morning when the boomerangs arrived. This time, however, there was a bit of explanation. First the flattery – how BHS under new management was a comeback story in its own right. Then Atkins charted the faltering history of their relationship with BHS, ending with a declaration of its determination, like Niki Lauda, 'to stage another comeback'. Then the card went for their one objective – a request for a meeting: 'Like BHS,

Atkins has changed. Like BHS, Atkins is a fun, lively, fashionable company. And great value for money . . .What a
partnership there could be! After all, which of your other
suppliers would go to these lengths to liven up your week?'
It worked. Andrew Freemen recalls: 'We got our phone call.
And that was all we wanted. A meeting, that is, with the
right background and tone to it.'

Everything about this case illustrates the power of creative
leadership. And there was no doubt that the issue was
squarely with the leader, both in Atkins and in their competitor companies. But the difference in leadership style
could not have been greater. People were running around
like headless chickens in all the affected suppliers. The
temptation for Atkins too was to act precipitously, but they
would never be more than a me-too in the face of stiff competition. A lot of leadership and courage was needed to hold
fire, and incubate the problem, when the competition were
already doing anything, and sparing no expense, to get their
contracts renewed. Quality thinking, not executive action,
was the secret. Andrew recognised the nuances of internal
politics, knowing that his message had to be got across at
several levels at the same time: 'If you go up one level of
management at a time, it is very difficult to continue up the
ladder if you are stopped at the level below.' And his strategy
resulted in real, tangible results. Literally millions of pounds
worth of business was salvaged and the company's uncertain
future was secured, in return for promotional expenditure
of less than a thousand pounds. The whole campaign was
based on an idea of Andrew Freeman's that he had used on
a smaller scale when MD of a previous company. This sort
of creativity is not the sole responsibility of the leader – far
from it. But the leader can be an example, and can help to
create an empowering culture that encourages others to add
their own unique blend of creativity.

MAKING DECISIONS
THAT COUNT

A lot of the leaders I met adopt the modest view that you need to get more than half your decisions right. I think the percentage required is in reality somewhat higher. But what is, perhaps, more important is the nature of decisions, and their impact on the business. A few notable good decisions can rocket a manager to the heights of leadership, whatever his or her hit rate. So how do leaders think when it comes to making decisions? Are there any lessons that aspiring business leaders can learn and apply?

Decision-making, like other aspects of management, has its left-brain and right-brain aspects. Sometimes making a decision will be nothing more than a careful and objective marshalling of the facts – the pros and cons of an argument, or the advantages and disadvantages of a course of action. This process calls on the left-brain logical, sequential form of reasoning that applies to a lot of routine decisions. But these kinds of decisions represent only a small proportion of those that have to be faced by the leader. They are typically handled by successive layers of managers lower down the company hierarchy, and are heavily reliant on systems, or computer programs. It can even be argued that decisions that do not require real judgement, or intuitive skill, should not even rank for inclusion in a manager's responsibility, let alone the company chief's.

A good decision-maker has to question the system, and the many assumptions upon which seemingly rational, logical conclusions have been based. This is where the intuitive, questioning, lateral thinking of the right brain comes into play. Who decides whether the data are complete and valid – especially projections about future revenues and costs upon which most capital investments stand or fall? What assumptions have been made throughout the many layers of data-gathering and analysis, and how valid are those assumptions? Are they in turn based on facts, opinions, judgements, beliefs, feelings, or prejudices? To what extent will key assumptions about interest rates or exchange rates, for example, change the outcome of the appraisal – and thus the decision? On what logical basis can a final go or no-go decision be made?

These sorts of judgements, upon which the best decisions are made, are the added value of good management, and a hallmark of leadership. Those that do it best see this aspect of decision-making as more of an art than a science. The ability to make good decisions, often on the basis of very incomplete information, sometimes within tight timescales, and without always being able to give 'logical' reasons, involves intuitive, courageous leadership.

Deciding to wait

It is considered part of the modern manager's function to make fast decisions, especially when insufficient data adds to the risk. It is positively macho to make *very* fast decisions, especially when being watched by admiring juniors, or parent company bosses. But it is not necessarily wise to do so, and most top leaders do not fall into the trap of making decisions before they have to be made. Frequently a major issue is overtaken, and even forgotten, by the time what was initially considered a deadline is reached. More frequently, during the period of apparent 'delay', more data come to hand which can improve the quality of a decision, or further useful analysis of the data is carried out. When a decision *has* to be made – and this again may involve judgement, and a sixth sense – however scanty the information, the true leader will not flinch from the responsibility.

Very few decisions cannot wait 24 hours, and this

particularly applies at the strategic end of the business, which rightly occupies the chairman or chief executive. An acquisition, for example, might take many months, or even years, to materialise, with a lot of expense and effort along the way. In this context, a day or two in further deliberation, or just doing nothing, will usually be adequately repaid, in quality of decision rather than macho image. Deciding to wait might itself be an important decision for the leader to make.

Working to deadlines

Leaders are quite familiar with working to deadlines, and have got where thay are today by meeting the important ones. But most decisions can wait. Sir Richard Greenbury, chairman of Marks & Spencer, will often leave a decision, especially an important one, until the following day. Usually this incubation period is enough for a clear decision to emerge in the light of a new day. Charles Mackay at Inchcape also knows what it is to sleep on a problem. Typically, a proposal received on a Friday will have a decision by the following Wednesday – whatever the level of information. But even he will defer the bigger decisions, not so much to obtain more data (as there are usually diminishing returns to this activity) but to rethink the issues. Essentially the 'delay' is a time for thinking, either consciously mulling over the issues, or, more frequently, allowing the subconscious to do its natural sorting out job, after which a decision emerges, and feels right.

Although the right brain does not acknowledge deadlines, and its incubation period can vary from a few moments to years, sometimes good decisions are linked to pressure and deadlines. Marion Lewis at Logica, for example, needs a deadline. An important report she has to write will wait until ominously close to the deadline, 'then it just flows'. I referred earlier to a decision Roger Burnell at Britannia

Airways had to make related to the retirement of one of the company's directors, but which had more far-reaching implications. In this case there was no pressing urgency, but he gave himself a 'private' deadline of spring 1994 to make the final decision – and, sure enough, his intuitive brain came up with the answer one sunny Sunday when he was mowing the lawn. He has learned to use the deadline as a device to stimulate his thinking. Mike Bett at BT, and other CEs I spoke with, also enjoy the pressure of a deadline. But the best deadline becomes internal to the leader, and reflects his or her own levels of motivation and stress, whilst at the same time building in the incubation period that the subconscious needs. And we are all different, so we need to know how and when we do our best thinking and make our best decisions, where necessary incorporating appropriate timescales into our goals.

Confidence in your decisions

Another aspect of decision-making is the confidence of knowing a decision is right, and this seems to apply whether decisions are made quickly or slowly. Some of those I met argued that this ability to make important decisions routinely, and trust one's judgement, is just the product of years of experience. Others recognise a sixth sense, an intuitive feeling of something being right or wrong. And this was more marked when the idea or decision just came out of the blue, after a period when it was not being consciously thought about.

As we saw earlier, Graham Cooper had a major problem solved 'for him' after sleeping on it. Although he had put plenty of conscious thought into the problem, the decision, when it finally came was, in effect, made for him. As well as a clear yes/no decision, he had, at the same time, a clearer perspective on the many issues involved. This was not a 'eureka' in the sense of a brand new line of thinking – he had gone over the many aspects of the case a hundred times – but a strong feeling about the *rightness* of what he had been unsure about the night before. Although there were plenty of problems associated with the decision (the right decision might well be the hardest one), the confidence that a right decision had been made made everything else seem possible, and secondary by comparison. So even a distasteful decision, perhaps involving many redundancies or a difficult personal situation, comes as a relief when you know it is right. The whole weight of the matter is then off your shoulders, as you turn a corner of confidence in your decision.

Richard Gooding of London Luton Airport was negotiating with a contractor contra claims against the airport following a major contract. The claim was for about £300,000; the value estimated by the airport was nearer £200,000. On this occasion, and quite contrary to normal practice, Richard felt strongly that he should settle at £300,000 rather than go through the usual months of horsetrading. This decision was based upon how he *felt* the other party would think and act, rather than the numbers themselves.

Contractor's claims and counter-claims are, of course, an example of everyday decision-making to which basic reasoning and logic are applied – all the pros and cons are weighed up, including some evaluation of unmeasurable or indirect factors. Richard's decision, as decisions go, was no big deal – the indirect costs of fighting for that £100,000 difference might easily have been greater than the amount saved, forgetting all the positive, money earning things he and his staff might be doing rather than endlessly arguing and creating animosity in an otherwise good relationship. But it was the feeling of *rightness* that added another dimension. Although quite amenable to conscious. logical reasoning, (unlike, perhaps, raw people judgements) contractual or financial decisions can also benefit from the sixth sense.

Few decisions involving large sums of money are free of subjective elements and unknowns. And these are the ones that filter upward to the leader. Somehow the subconscious mind can see the picture more holistically, is not stuck to rigid principles or past practice, can cope with the softer 'people' aspects, and seems far more perceptive than the left side of the brain in looking to the future.

This feeling of 'rightness', often of complete certainty, is part of the nonverbal, non-logical right brain way of thinking. It is a recurring feature in important decisions, which, it seems, are not necessarily based on any recognisable logic. Leon King, managing director of Fosroc Expandite, stresses the importance of this leadership skill when choosing consultants, where it is vital to work with mutual trust. Paul Southworth at Avon Cosmetics also had to call on this intuitive decision-making skill when engaging advertising consultants. In that case the small firm presenting as part of a 'beauty contest' could not compete in any typical track record or credentials sense. But there was something about both the young presenter and the ideas put forward for a campaign that evoked a sense of certainty which, for Paul, made a decision to go with them inevitable.

This leadership skill is used for all sorts of decisions. It might take Ian Dixon of Willmott Dixon between ten minutes and half an hour to decide to close a company, but this intuitive skill has had to be practised and developed. David Webster, deputy chairman of the Argyll Group, is no stranger to decision-making. He recalls viewing a hotel on a Friday and signing a contract for its purchase on the Sunday. Such decisions might be made in volume by the leader, depending on the nature of the business. But what makes this sort of experience scary, with hindsight as well as at the time, when adrenaline is flowing freely, is the ripple effect of many such decisions, which can affect the very direction of the business. The hotel deal David Webster struck was to become a strategic turning point in the whole business. The cumulative effect of decisions, coupled with the tendency for the difficult decisions to rise to the top of the hierarchy (where the buck stops) make the art of decision-making an important feature of leadership.

TIPS FOR TOMORROW'S LEADERS

1. Spend plenty of time thinking consciously about your problem or decision, from every possible angle.

2. Live with frustration – sometimes it is the seed of a great idea, and in any case is a part of leadership.

3. If you get stuck on a problem, do something completely different – forget about it.

4. Don't be weak in accepting unnecessary deadlines, or giving yourself them. That's the road to ulcers.

5. Check out even the most brilliant ideas. Use others who will also be responsible for implementation.

6. Every so often, state and restate your main goals and problems, including personal ones. This registers them with your unconscious so it can work on them while you are busy with something else.

7. Don't copy specific promotional ideas. They never seem to work the second time round. Dream up your own, as Andrew Freeman did.

8. Make decisions based on how you feel as well as what you think.

9. Be wary of systems or data that dictate what you have to do. You are always responsible for your own decisions. Leaders change systems and question data if necessary.

10. Don't make fast decisions unless you really have to. Be prepared to sleep on a decision. It might be overtaken by events tomorrow, or you might see things in a different light. You will be remembered for right decisions rather than fast ones.

11. Recall the circumstances in which you have made your best decisions. It may have been during a short break away from work, first thing in the morning, during the night when you felt you could not sleep, or sitting in the park opposite the office. Use and develop the best personal environment and circumstances for quality decisions.

12. When making decisions about people, note particularly your feelings, even if you cannot express them, and also take account of first impressions. Don't depend on CVs, references, opinions, or psychometric tests – just give them their fair place. Have the courage to form your own, unique impression of a person. That's part of leading.

13. Welcome and enjoy having to make decisions. They are what make you what you are, and you can't avoid them if you want to make anything of yourself.

14. Get to know your inbuilt mechanism that helps you to make the best decisions – your wise, inner friend and adviser. It's not difficult. Simply stop doing things for long enough to hear what is going on inside, and make some personal space for yourself.

$$\boxed{5}$$

Living Like a Leader

THERE ARE SURPRISINGLY few workaholics right at the top. Sir Richard Greenbury, chairman of Marks & Spencer, insists on taking a full three weeks' holiday, during which he reads avidly, and the business has also got to fit in with his passion for tennis. Sir Malcolm Field, group chief executive of W H Smith, admits he is a 'bit of a workaholic' but doesn't think about work on holiday. 'The workaholic', says Derek Williams at CCSB 'lives on the job. The job lives with the leader.'

For just about every leader I met, there was life beyond business. Their descriptions of non-work activities left me marvelling at the time management ingenuity of some of these top leaders. Sir Robert Evans, former chairman of British Gas, spent some 18 months on a major garden pond project which sounded close to a full-time job for lesser mortals

All this does not mean that the business is not high in any leader's personal order of priority, nor that work does not evoke enthusiasm, commitment and passion on the part of the leader. The leader in almost every case has a meaningful life outside the business or organisation, important in its quality, if not in the proportion of waking hours it comprises. This might show up in humble and unremarkable pastimes and interests that belie a lofty business position and influence. There seems to be a balance between a potentially all-consuming but mentally restricting business

life, and the relative normality but mental or spiritual richness of private life. Managing people and organisations can
be absorbing at any level – clockwatching is one phenomenon that does not affect the leader.

WORK AND LEISURE

The work ethic is still strong, especially at the age typical of
the top leaders I interviewed. So even when absorbed by the
job, and commanding in some cases pop star earnings, most
could still talk of work and leisure in distinct terms. But
there is an increasing trend in business towards automation
and reduced employment, and a growing emphasis on
leisure and recreation. If hardly a new phenomenon, leisure
is becoming more and more significant, occupying a bigger
part of each person's life. This, of course, applies to staff at
all levels, and reflects the changing pattern of employment
that Charles Handy and others have written about, with
long-term unemployment, flexible employment with part-
time working, increasing self-employment and subcontracting, and fast-changing technology.

Definitions of both 'work' and 'leisure' have special significance in the case of the top management of a company.
The boss is still stereotyped as conducting business deals on
the golf course, returning late from business lunches, and
flying off to exotic places. So I was interested to know how
leaders viewed so-called work and so-called leisure, and the
distinctions they made between them. Differing so much
from person to person, these concepts, steeped in personal
history and career background, are just the frames of mind
we adopt. So which frame of mind is better for sound
decisions, creativity and the unique responsibilities of top
leadership? How hard do the top business leaders work,
and how do they find time for a meaningful private life?

BE YOUR OWN PERSON

What is meant by work and leisure varies from worker to worker and manager to manager. The distinction is important to most top managers, who tend to value highly their favourite sports, hobbies and private time, recognising the benefits of a full out-of-work life. They don't like to consider themselves 'owned' by the company, or by anyone. So, whilst products of the corporation and its culture, as any other manager, they need not be corporate animals. On the contrary, as leaders, they tend to be their own person. Although their diaries might belie the fact, they have far greater freedom to order their work lives than a shop-floor or nine-to-five office worker. But at the same time the work/leisure distinction, at least at the edges, can be blurred.

It is hard sometimes for others – or indeed the leaders themselves – to know whether they are 'at work' or in leisure time. Modern business ensures that this distinction cannot be based on the clock. Even junior managers soon forget what a normal nine-to-five day means. Whole evenings and weekends can be taken up by more senior managers on semi-social company affairs.

But the distinction, at any level, is important. Whether you *feel* you are working, or enjoying leisure will affect your behaviour and performance. A person who is known to be specially creative, or who takes on special leadership qualities in some social or domestic context, might well be quite nondescript at work. Another person may only seem to shine in a work setting. Each views work and leisure differently, and they turn their creativity and motivation on and off with the transition to and from each mode. So this is the startling paradox: one person loves and the other person hates the very same aspects of either work or leisure. In the extreme one person dreads leaving for work in the morning, and another dreads leaving for home at night. And these feelings seem to be strangely connected with whether we perceive ourselves to be working or enjoying our private time, rather than what we are actually doing, where we are, or what time of day it is. As a leader, what may set you apart is that you have come to know yourself, how you think and how you achieve your goals, and how both work and non-work fit into your wider life. At the same time you carry on going for your goals, whether in work or leisure mode.

WORK OR LEADERSHIP?

At the highest level, work tends to be absorbing and stimulating – time flies. The accompanying pressures can be pleasurable, as they involve facing new challenges and solving problems. This mental stimulation and personal fulfilment is one of the less visible perks of being at the top. Yet from a lower vantage point the leader's role is hardly viewed as 'work' at all. Less predictably, some of the leaders I interviewed spoke of feeling an irrational guilt about enjoying their work as if it were leisure, while being handsomely rewarded into the bargain.

This work-ethic kind of guilt can also set in when you are not doing anything – or appear not to be. *Thinking*, of course, to the modern, macho business executive, means doing nothing. You are paid to *do*, not to *think*. The practice of reflective thinking has not yet penetrated western managerial culture – at least not during office hours. One MD confessed that, to this day, he cannot bring himself to spend too long just gazing out of his office window, however lofty or business-related his thoughts, and whatever power comes with his position. A similar sense of guilt, or even of mild failure, can result from a blank spot in the diary. So the leader will – knowingly or unknowingly – bring to work his personal philosophy of work and leisure, about what it *means* to be a leader, about the leader's role and how others see it, about himself as a person, and how others see him. This self-understanding provides some of the secrets of success.

Nowadays the importance of leisure is widely accepted – not just because of the economic reality of less work to go round, and shorter working hours, but as a factor in better performance and output through more contented and ful-filled people. The trend towards devolution of responsibility brings with it a respect for the individual, and in some com-panies the fostering of varied and fulfilling outside interests. Archie Norman at Asda, the retail chain, introduced poli-cies which positively encourage out-of-work activities. Such an attitude would have seemed patronising and intrusive not many years ago. It is now less acceptable to take work home regularly, with some employers viewing it as counterproduc-tive, a sign of managerial weakness rather than strength. Some of the business leaders I met have a personal policy of not taking work home. They value their leisure time. One way or another, most at least have a policy about this and other aspects of their work and private life.

A LEISURE MENTALITY

Flexible working hours and the practice of many larger groups to encourage and sponsor social activities add to the two-way traffic between work and leisure. Whilst the bound-aries have become increasingly unclear, the distinction is as important as ever, when people's perceptions, attitudes and behaviour are considered. When work *feels* more like leisure we work better. When leisure begins to feel like work, we don't seem to do as well in that.

Cultural and mental barriers do exist around work and

leisure, and unless we come to terms with our own definitions and priorities, we might well lose out on both. Talking
to the leaders, it does seem as if a 'leisure mentality' can
actually improve professional decision-making and creativity. If a more relaxed, unstressed approach is taken in the
corridors of power, whilst at the same time 'work thinking'
is allowed to encroach on sacred 'leisure time', there can be
benefits both ways. A lot more creative brainpower can be
released. Trying to suppress ideas that come to mind on a
Sunday morning can be as counterproductive as trying to
force creativity within the structure of a busy office life.
That's the way the brain seems to work.

THE WORK ENVIRONMENT

A big factor in the work/leisure distinction is the office or
workplace itself, and the effect this has on creativity. When
discussing what environment was conducive to the greatest
creativity, the same answer kept coming up, in different
guises: 'Not here' (gesturing around the spacious office
suite), or 'last place' (John Billing, Courtaulds Textiles) was
the typical response. Robert Ayling, British Airways CE,
said he would be happy for his office to be rented out, for
the amount of time he spends in it. And this fits well the
trend of MBWA – management by walking about. I suppose
the ivory tower office is the only place that is out of bounds,
under a leadership style that keeps in touch with staff and
customers. Roger Burnell, CE of Britannia Airways 'need[s]
to get out of the office, and talk to people', adding that he
does this much more now than ten years ago.

So while managers become increasingly remote and physically isolated as they climb through the ranks – although
there are fewer ranks to climb following the mass delayering
of most industries – the leader has to somehow reverse the

process. Jack Rowell, England rugby union manager and former MD of Golden Wonder – a people-man through and through – gets 'bored restless' in the office. The leader's immediate environment seems to induce mental atrophy, presumably with its associations with the left brain organisation, deadlines, interruptions, and reactive, conscious thinking. It tends to stifle any great leaps of thought and inspiration. So the movement away from the ivory tower to where the people are reflects and affects how present leaders *think*, and is part of their success.

Creating leisure mode in the office

Now and again the initial response I got suggested something different was happening in the office. Vernon Sankey at Reckitt and Colman produces plenty of clear, and often creative thinking right there in his office, with its pleasant view over the River Thames. But on further enquiry it transpired that these times of quality thought are in the morning, long before other staff have arrived and before the invasions of normal office hours and diary commitments. So a quasi-leisure mode seems to be possible, when the workplace can become, for a while, a private, relaxing environment that helps rather than hinders free thinking.

David Quarmby at Sainsbury's gets similar benefit from an informal evening session with one or two colleagues, which seems to be far more productive than any structured nine-to-five setting. So the physical workplace is not as significant as the mental state of the leader, and his *associations* with wherever he happens to be. Usually the office has an association of *doing* rather than *thinking* (in any deep or creative sense), and rarely allows the personal uninterrupted 'space' that the creative mind needs. And the modern always-open-door policy (which must rank as *the* most misguided time management policy – but that's another story) makes it so much more difficult to budget for vital thinking time. So the widespread experience of the country's top business leaders is that, however paradoxical and wasteful of fancy head office resources, good ideas inside the company premises are the exception rather than the rule.

Wayne Murcar, then Director and GM of the British Pipeline Agency, who sadly died recently, would spend two to three hours each day thinking, which he claimed was the prime role of the chief in maintaining direction. His leadership policy was a brave one as his office was on the ground floor in full view of staff coming and going, who had come to accept their sleeping boss. Like many other leaders with an individual style of thinking and behaviour, he had earned the respect that allowed him to do what he felt was right. An abundance of creative ideas was the outcome of his seemingly passive style. So, an office *can* be a hotbed of new thinking and innovation. It is more likely, however, to be the engine room of a left brain bureaucratically inclined organisation which stultifies novel thought. To the mind, the work environment is associated with work, and the state of mind it induces.

Offices and non-offices

If this tendency to office sterility is not corrected naturally, it might be tackled more fundamentally. Although Archie Norman at Asda has an office, it is far from the average CEO's hideout. He 'occupies' the corner of a large, open plan office, with other staff present. His desk, he insists, is just somewhere to put the telephone. Archie's is certainly no conventional CEO's office, insulated from the coal-face of the business, and this directly reflects his policy of putting people first. The immediate team sharing floorspace include support for the thousands of suggestions from staff that are carefully processed each year. So the chief executive's office was transformed into what felt, to me, like a communication centre and innovation clearing house.

Mike Jackson, MD of Birmingham Midshires Building Society took it all a stage further. I met him in a sort of foyer/lounge area in one of their buildings and Mike turned up with a canvas bag, a mobile telephone, and a few other belongings, having made his own way, as I had done, to the venue. It transpired he has no office. As part of a major change involving new open plan offices, and a very open culture, he is leading the way by personal example. For Mike, MBWA and all the benefits of keeping in very close touch with the company and its customers have been structured into his very way of life.

To say that the leaders' policies of personal office accommodation varied a lot would be an understatement. In some cases the chairman and CEO seemed to occupy a whole floor of the building, making all sorts of personal statements through layout, furnishings, works of art, security and so on. Barry Dale, Group CE of the Littlewoods group scrapped an outside expert's plan for a complete head office refurbishment, at a very advanced stage, as it did not reflect the open culture he wanted to create from the top of the company. Whatever the colour of the walls, and despite the token informality and 'creative environment' many bosses attempt to create by furnishing and seating layout, the irony cannot be avoided – the big ideas usually come somewhere else.

Usually a building mirrors the whole bureaucracy and hierarchy of a company, and accentuates divisions. As though functions themselves did not create enough barriers, the creative synergy that only comes from mixing people from different backgrounds is lost to the business. Serious attempts at devolving authority and an open creative culture usually start with getting the physical accommodation right.

Thereafter, the message from hundreds of discussions was that the leader, and his managers, might just spend too much time in the office.

Getting outside the office

Mental sterility in the office corrects itself in other ways. As so many of the leaders spent long periods away from the office, visiting plants, retail outlets, or outside organisations, the seeming barrenness of the ivory tower did not take its toll. Frequent travel provides its own opportunities for private space, a measure of relaxation, and free thinking. In some cases a CEO would get out of the office for short periods to blow out some cobwebs, or to stop getting bogged down in detail. Marion Lewis at Logica has long since learned the value of a short walk in the park nearby, to let her mind do its best and get in the right frame of mind for any demands of the job. It seems that mega problems can dissolve miraculously during a 20 minute constitutional, especially if the weather is kind. Nature contributes its unique sights, smells and sounds, and the brain switches to its 'out of office' mode. These mental breaks can become life or death at the top management level, but are often scheduled out of busy lives. Yet walking round the block can cause the same irrational guilt as passively thinking in the office. During work time, the boss of one world-leading group relies entirely on visits to the washroom for his creativity and the maintenance of his sanity. But the treadmill of business life demands that any opportunities for change that do arise, such as travel, must be grasped before other demands press in.

Executive floor inspiration

Several chiefs echoed Roger Burnell at Britannia Airways, who rarely ever does any really creative thinking inside his own office. In many other cases, executive floor inspiration was a rare event, which happened by default. For instance, a chairman or chief executive might get a good idea during a meeting, even though the idea would bear no direct relation to the subject of the meeting, but might have been triggered by a chance remark. Or it might come during a period of daydreaming (a regular therapeutic indulgence of many top executives inclined to right brain thinking, and championed by Derek Williams, the dynamic MD of CCSB,) in almost any meeting or group setting. Similarly, if a novel idea comes while reading a report, the chances are, again, that the idea will have no direct link with the subject of the report. This is not to suggest that no ideas or questions come consciously while reading a report, or when taking part in a meeting, but rather that, on reflection, the best ideas – the quality thinking, if you like – seem to be of the uninvited kind. By their very nature, the issues addressed will not appear on any formal agenda or carefully planned 'to do' list.

The fertile brain seems to work in this anarchic but effective way, regardless of time and place. Mike Jackson at Birmingham Midshires Building Society recalls listening patiently to a presentation in his office (when he had one) on some human resources topic. He has no recollection of the details of the presentation, but well recalls the brainwave of an idea that came to his mind in the soporific haze of the long presentation – a brainwave not connected (in any conscious way) to the subject in hand. As he describes it, 'I didn't know what I was looking for' – but he found it all the same.

No doubt some tenuous link could be traced to a word or idea that had triggered his mind, or maybe he was just in his own private world of thought. Either way, the brain, at least when left free to do so, seems to do what is best, and addresses what it decides are the important issues, often taking us by surprise. The alarming reality is that managers are effective *despite* structures, monthly meetings and systems. The mind will create its own non-work environment, given half a chance, and produce quality thoughts without conscious effort. The leadership secret is to know what is happening, and the circumstances that make for better thinking, and then to trust and use the insights that arise. Middle managers might get away with using half their brain. Top leaders, it seems, do not.

The office can take on a mysterious creativity at weekends, providing the same thinking haven as an early morning or late night session. So the perception of leisure rather than work, and the relaxed mental state it brings, rather than the physical working environment, is what opens up the creative subconscious. But most weekends are spent away from work, and, as it happens, most creativity occurs outside the office – at home, in the garden, when travelling, or anywhere the mind can do a bit of freewheeling. We need to see, therefore, how the leader lives outside the business.

CREATIVITY IN LEISURE MODE

Where does work stop, and leisure begin for the busy leader? And what is the significance of the boundaries, or lack of them, for leaders and would-be leaders? Most top business leaders are familiar with the treadmill of a long working day, which is often a price to pay when climbing through the middle and senior management ranks. And old habits die hard. Although the demands at board level preclude a normal nine to five routine, or indeed any routine, I met few leaders with one-track company minds. It was surprisingly common for the CE of a multimillion pound group to be able to switch off at the end of a day, and weekends and holidays were often quite sacred. On the other hand, John Welsby, CE of British Rail, uses 'wet Sundays' as an excuse to hide away in his study and do some 'serious thinking' – enjoying, nonetheless, the creativity and productivity of leisure mode. Richard Gooding at London Luton Airport credits his Saturday or Sunday baths with maximum creativity. It was when having one Saturday morning bath that he put together a major restructuring, which solved some important personnel issues. Confine a senior manager to his office, and you may have a colourless shadow of a leader, and an impoverished business into the bargain.

It seems that the higher a manager rises, and the greater the job pressures, the more important it is for him or her to maintain a private life and non-business interests, which seem to be more valued with the passing of years. This ability to switch off is more important, it appears, than the length of the working week. However clearly defined an individual's career might be, managerial longevity seems to be more linked to a balanced lifestyle and effective thinking (being smart, or wise, if you like) than to narrow single-mindedness. Left brain managers get so far, sometimes very quickly, but then get weeded out – usually because of a lack of followership upon which their performance relies – before they reach the top. Few of the leaders I met had always valued their private lives as they now do, or had managed to balance their priorities, the change coming relatively late in their careers. In the same evolutionary way, most had come to rely more on intuition than cold logic and analysis.

But even those who could wind down on a Friday night could not shut out the business completely. Most did not attempt to, having experienced so many valuable business ideas coming during non-work time. Just as when in a board meeting or travelling the mind will not be tied to time and place, so ideas can and do come at any time in the evening and at weekends.

Many of the leaders I met were considerably more creative away from work than in the office – particularly when they managed to wind down and relax, or were engaged in an activity completely different from their usual work. The danger is that, away from your secretary and the trappings of the business, ideas are not captured and used. Even worse, that lifestyle discourages such thinking or suppresses intuition. Somehow, as a leader, you have to get this right. You are a leader because of what you are, including the way you think, rather than just because of what you *do* in your formal role. The business stays part of your 'circle of lifespace', as Derek Williams described it, wherever you happen to be.

Some of our unplanned, leisure-mode thoughts turn out to be the most significant for the business. And this is where the importance of a personal work/leisure strategy comes in. A happy partnership between work and private life is matched by the partnership of left brain, conscious thought, most of which occurs in the work environment, and right brain unconscious thinking, most of which, it seems, happens when we are, at least mentally, outside the business and its associations.

Nocturnal creativity

The leader's non-work life includes whatever hours of sleep he or she can get away with. The great majority of those I met valued their beauty sleep highly, and could not attribute their success to any Thatcher-like four or five hours of sleep a night. But their somnal indulgence allowed for the occasions when they would awake with an idea, or have to sacrifice any further sleep to a whirring mind.

A popular time for creative thoughts, especially those of the eureka variety, is about three o'clock in the morning.

This is not to suggest that top business people are insomniacs, although some get away with very little regular sleep. Indeed, many CEOs valued the fact that they were sound sleepers, whatever daytime problems they were facing. But they might still find themselves waking up during the night every few weeks, presented with an idea or line of thought that seemed to come out of the blue, and which in some cases solved a major current issue they were facing. These waking-up times produce some of the most significant ideas in British business. Business textbooks do not give this widespread phenomenon a moment's attention.

But nocturnal thinking takes different forms. Sometimes the whole episode will last just a few minutes – long enough for the thought to be gratefully registered in the conscious mind and, in the case of those who still smart from an earlier forgotten brainwave, scribbled down on a handy pad. The grateful sound sleeper will then go back to sleep. In other cases the night becomes an unending mental kaleidoscope in which important issues are pondered, memories explored, scenarios imagined, options evaluated and problems are solved. This might occur every few weeks, or days or months, depending often on what the company is going through and whether personal matters are pressing. Although this is conscious mental work, the state of physical relaxation and personal 'space' usually means that the right brain is brought into play, so that plenty of insights and creative ideas can be thrown into the melting pot, along with the less pleasant worrying that we all do so well in the small hours. Although these sessions might not produce a memorable eureka, they will often clarify and simplify pressing issues, so that you are better able to face them in the light of another day. The big lesson, of course, is not to fight what your brain seems determined to do.

Night-time mental blitzes are a regular part of Derek Williams's life, so he has come to value a spare bed. Keith

Henry at Brown and Root is a definite three o'clock person and has long since learned to always keep a notepad and pen within reach. Sir Nicholas Goodison, TSB chairman, matches exactly this popular three o'clock nocturnal profile. Grant Rabey, MD of RS Components, also values the 'wee hours of the morning'. Sir Ralph Robins, chairman of Rolls-Royce, is a 3.30 to 4.00 person, and he is fortunate enough to be able to remember his ideas.

Keith Oates at Marks & Spencer is also prolific in night-time ideas, which are usually recalled at some time during the following day. He has come to trust his memory, as well as the value of the ideas themselves. Others have to rack their brains the following day, and sometimes a brilliant idea is lost. Robert Wilson at RTZ is another three o'clock person who is liable to forget his night-time revelations. Ken Whittaker, MD of Hoogovens, excels mentally at one o'clock on Sunday mornings. So night-time can be a favourite time of day.

Sir John Hoskyns, chairman of the Burton group, as well as waking from time to time in the middle of the night with useful ideas, also values the time just before going to sleep, referring to the importance of mental images 'just before consciousness'. Sir David Alliance, chairman of Coats Viyella, has developed the habit of thinking over the issues that affect him each night before going to sleep. The time immediately before sleep, when the brain runs at slow 'alpha' wavelengths, is a good time to do mental housekeeping, which acts as a sort of instruction to the sleeping brain to sort out and solve things – resulting in middle of the night eurekas or a new, clearer perspective in the morning. But Friday – and this illustrates the interesting work/leisure personal distinction – is Sir David's night off from thinking.

Then the pattern moves to daylight, and the new morning. Bob Hawley at Nuclear Electric will wake very early and scribble down as many as half a dozen ideas. Robert

Solberg, deputy chairman of Texaco Ltd, also comes to life
mentally in the early morning, sometimes after a light, trou-
bled sleep. If he doesn't capture ideas then, the chances are
they will come while he is showering. Michael Wemms at
Tesco is another early morning person who knows the benefits of literally sleeping on a problem. All the evidence is that
things are so much clearer after a good night's sleep – as
though the mind has not stopped working on the matter,
and has presented its findings and solutions. Peter Smith at
Marconi talks about 'randomised thoughts' coming perhaps
20 minutes after waking, triggering some half a dozen new
problems, questions or angles on the subjects. He modestly
attributes to these morning thinking periods a 'large number' of good ideas. Keith Oates will use his morning clarity
to visualise the events of the coming day, such as an important meeting. This mental rehearsal seems to be a very
effective form of preparation, which cannot be done in a
structured, left brain way, and first thing in the morning is a
popular time for it.

All this exemplifies the part that unconscious thought
processes play in our lives, without reference to office buildings or hours. This is the intuitive leader at large. But these
out-of-office insights do have a significant effect on the business. They are how the leader lives as a total person, rather
than fulfilling a narrow role in the boardroom or in a negotiating session. And, although unobserved, and hardly understood – even by the leader himself – they seem to account
for some of his top leadership qualities.

PERSONAL THINKING CLOCKS

The idea of personal clocks is not a new one, and this is
another aspect of the wider personal context of the leader.
We each seem to be able to do things better at certain times

of the day, which vary from person to person – hence our descriptions of a 'morning person' or a 'night person'. But we will probably find we have clocks that differ when we consider *thinking* rather than *doing*. More than this, the time and place that are best for conscious, left brain thinking (perhaps a structured work setting) are likely to differ from those that produce more open, creative right brain thinking. In terms of quality thinking, we are almost certainly resorting to the right brain when new perspectives, or what is termed lateral thought, is conceived.

Most significant changes in business tend to originate with this sort of thinking, and important breakthroughs in science, medicine and other non-business areas have followed a similar pattern. Quantum insights rather than incremental thought steps tend to call on the whole brain; a person who has recognised and accommodated this fact is likely to produce the quality thinking that gives the edge. In terms of personal clocks, therefore, a 20 minute morning reverie or relaxing, scenic car journey might be of far greater value than a carefully scheduled slot of office day. As we have seen, place as well as time is a factor, as is the highly personal association of work or leisure, pleasure or pain. Most of the leaders I met have managed to bring intuitive, creative, right brain thinking into the habits, attitudes and values that make up their total life. Before working out how others think, get to know your own thinking style and personal clock.

MENTAL BRIDGES BETWEEN WORK AND LEISURE

The journey to and from the office can be important, offering a mental bridge between work and leisure. And

the car seems to beat the boardroom for producing winning business ideas. Scores of leaders have recounted how
much of their best thinking takes place while they are
travelling. Derek Drake has come to rely on his one-and-
a-half-hour drive to the office as prime thinking time.
Andrew Michel, then MD of FKI Babcock Robey, refuses
to live less than three-quarters of an hour's driving time
from his work, as he finds the time so valuable. This is not
just a time when the mind can mull over issues in a kind
of neutral gear, but it is an opportunity for winding up
and winding down, a welcome buffer between business
and private life. In the morning, all the forthcoming issues
will be gone over in the mind, a rough plan for the day
agreed, forthcoming decisions considered, and any ideas
gratefully registered for later use. At the same time, pressing domestic and other personal issues might perhaps be
thought about then discarded, so that a productive state of
mind for work is achieved, uncluttered by home and social
matters. The reverse will happen in the evening, as important business issues of the day are reviewed then mentally
filed away, and both mind and body adapt in the transition back to leisure mode. Although not a universal practice, this illustrates the way in which the limbo time spent
travelling is used to help create a balanced life.

Dr Mike Lloyd, MD of GEC Alsthom Transport, had
been going over a logistical reorganisation in his mind for
some time. After many meetings and discussions he was
uncomfortable with the proposed plans; they did not seem
to fit. But, said Mike, during a two-hour car journey to
Rugby a very simple strategy 'just seemed to come into
my mind'. This resulted in a major restructuring involving
factory locations, with big economic benefits. So routine
car journeys, as well as allowing time to sort out your
thoughts, also produce eureka type flashes of insight. This
is not the car as an extension of the office – for many

leaders the car easily beats the office as a creative environment.

Interestingly, those CEs and chairmen who are driven by chauffeur did not experience anything like the benefits their driving colleagues did. Even a silent chauffeur or passenger can undo the private space associated with this creative, neutral gear kind of mobile thinking. In one case, switching off the light in the car was the signal for the chauffeur not to interrupt the chairman's reverie. But more often than not, when the CEO was being driven, the car was likely to be a simple extension of the office, where paperwork is cleared, telephone work is done and routine decisions made. This does not make for creativity, it just extends the operational conscious thinking part of the leader's life, with its 'diminishing returns'. So lower tier managers need not envy their bosses' chauffeur-driven journeys to work if effective leadership is what they aspire to.

Mobile and car telephones are a love-hate issue. Some of the leaders refused to use one, to safeguard the uninterrupted privacy and thinking time a car journey afforded, and the useful ideas it produced. Conversely, another CEO, not wanting to risk a great idea being forgotten, would never let the phone out of his reach in case an idea came to him, so he could then telephone the appropriate manager. In each case, however different the approach, the journey is not 'wasted' time, and in most cases good *thinking* time is valued more highly than good *doing* time. Travelling times are a chance for free thinking that is anticipated with pleasure. Radios are no problem for most, and the combination of a long motorway drive and the car radio can just about guarantee Richard Gooding a fruitful journey. In some cases fascinating, semiconscious associations have been triggered from the radio. In other cases it helps towards the relaxed state of mind that induces creative thinking.

Longer journeys

Of course most bosses have plenty of opportunity for travel apart from the home to work journey. Long car, train or plane trips afford plenty of time for a more reflective way of life. And sure enough, such journeys turn out to be extremely productive. Brian Maguire of Golden West Foods pinpoints one memorable eureka concerning their flour ferment system to a long train journey, when he was thinking about something else. His comments also illustrate how forceful analogies can be in thinking. 'It was as if each piece of information on trial represented a different symbol on a fruit machine, and, no matter how often I played the machine, I could never get the winning combination. It appears that, unbeknown to me, my brain was a gambler, and suddenly came up with the winning line. But what is most important is that, having done so, it made my conscious mind aware of the answer.' He adds, more generally, that 'flashes of inspiration often don't initially appear to have relevance, but the more one investigates and challenges them, the more one realises their true value.' The fact that such insights can come during a routine train journey, rather than on expensive brainstorming weekends or in a board meeting, should reassure any aspiring leader.

In some cases, important reports or speeches have been produced during the relatively relaxed, uninterrupted hours of a long flight or rail journey. Sir Ralph Robins, chairman of Rolls-Royce, dates the main creative work for what turned out to be one of the biggest single projects in British engineering to a long flight. And Paul Southworth at Avon Cosmetics came up with a radical new marketing concept on a US flight. Grant Raby, MD of RS Components, was on a plane trip back from a 'boring' conference in Toronto when some major ideas regarding supply chain management took shape. Although the concept was quite familiar, its application to his company, and in particular ways to communicate it and bring about the changes, came as a true inspiration; even a boring conference can produce the seed of an idea. But the real creativity happens inside you when you are in mental freewheeling mode. And travel, resented by many, seems to be a popular thought-promoting activity, given the right attitude. Indeed, it has been found to be more conducive to innovative thinking than any other time or situation in the workplace schedule.

Autopilot

The characteristics of free-wheeling thought, especially when driving, are fascinating. What I heard, time and time again, was how after a long car journey hardly a crossing, roundabout or village is remembered. Most 'natural' drivers are very familiar with this phenomenon. 'I seem to be driving on autopilot' was the common description. The mind is totally absorbed in what it is thinking about, and quite unconscious of the 'here and now' of the journey or the complexities of the actual driving process. Miraculously, we don't seem to hit things, and are quickly brought back to the 'here and now' by even subtle signals that might spell danger or the need for caution, then we settle back into our private world of thought.

These freewheeling thinking sessions, when no particular problem or issue is being addressed, but the mind just seems to wander freely, are very valuable times for getting new ideas and solving problems. Frequently we can put the world and company to rights on a long enough journey, especially if driving through pleasant countryside in good weather and in leisurely style. These journeys do not necessarily produce the eurekas that one gets in completely relaxing times, such as when pottering about in the garden, or listening to a musical concert, or perhaps on a train journey. But there can be plenty of insights, and the mind is amazingly productive in getting through a lot of issues, both work and personally related. Many of the leaders I spoke to had experienced this sort of thinking, and their business had benefited. Some had learned, through long experience, the importance of choosing the best 'thinking routes', and not cutting their timing so tight as to make driving and the stress of reaching deadlines tie up their mind.

Choosing priorities

On these occasions the mind seems to choose its own priorities. It decides, if you like, what it should bring next to our awareness. For this reason a social or domestic matter – something that, at least subconsciously, is a current problem or issue – might invade the consideration of a business issue – and vice versa. A few of the CEOs who are fit enough to do regular jogging describe a very similar thinking pattern to the car drive. Jeffrey Herbert, CE of Charter plc, a keen jogger, talks about a 'selection process' in which his mind is occupied by issues 'not known in advance'. Frank Turner, MD of of Lucas Aerospace, when running half marathons, 'can see a greater order to things, and sometimes come[s] up with inspirational thoughts.' Thoughts emerging from the subconscious seem to come in some *order* which, although seeming at the time quite random, upon reflection seems to reveal some sort of priority ranking – some sense. This phenomenon – a flow of thoughts in some personally meaningful order – is applied in a number of situations, generally where an activity can be carried out 'without thinking', in the same way as driving on 'autopilot'. So gentle sailing, for example, at least for an experienced sailor, would foster similar creativity, as it seems does golf when played without an opponent. All this happens without our trying. But, even more remarkable, the sense and purpose rising from the unconscious mind might be more truthful and useful than any logical attempt to achieve priority ranking. That is, it also does a better job.

So not only does the right brain arrange *what* we think about during these free thinking sessions, but it will also sort out the order to best cater for our overall psychological welfare. This right-brain-free thinking is so natural a skill that these leaders hardly recognised it as a factor in their success – 'Doesn't everybody use their time in this way?' The answer, sadly, is no. Most managers, not recognising just how the right side of the brain best works, unknowingly plan such thinking opportunities out of their lives. Travel is seen as a waste of valuable working time, so the objective is to get there fast, even if the route is harder on the nerves, and you have to concentrate on getting there intact rather than in peak mental state. Or, with superior, instinctive driving skill, the car becomes a secondary office, and telephone communication is hardly disrupted.

In its standard executive form, a long journey by train or plane, although an ideal opportunity for free creative thinking, is also likely to be filled with more conscious, left brain, work-mode activity. Time management wisdom says that you fill up such 'gaps' by always having work with you. Such a work mentality will inevitably impact on a manager's private life, with consequences that might affect health, relationships and other important interests, and will almost certainly be counterproductive in terms of true productivity in the business and longer term career. The dangers of stress are well known, of course. But few managers appreciate just how their total lifestyle can affect their management ability and leadership potential. Simple changes in how we live can have a big effect on what we achieve. True leaders learn a better way, before time and physical health run out.

THE LEADER AT PLAY

So far I have addressed what I term the leisure mentality which most of us are familiar with when winding down from a busy work day, and putting our feet up, or embarking on a journey when we can be ourselves and are free to think or not think as we please. In its narrower sense, however, leisure is more to do with the pastimes, sports and the non-work interests that we engage in. And even though these might be very absorbing in their own right – sometimes as demanding as anything we cope with at 'work' – they are nonetheless ripe for invading by valuable creative thought which might well relate to the business. Whether fly fishing for trout (Sir John Hoskyns, Burtons), in the darkroom developing photographs (Lord Young, Cable and Wireless), or in the greenhouse (Bob Nice, Ratcliff Tail Lifts), leaders find a welcome relaxation and pleasure that adds to their success as people and leaders.

Walking, and to a lesser extent jogging, was a favourite pastime for the executives in the age range represented in our research. Frank Davies, now retired from Rockware, learned over the years how to keep mentally in top form for leadership, walking and tenting on Offas Dike. Sir Anthony Gill, chairman of Lucas, owes much of his creativity to his hobby of sailing, a time he says, for BGOs – blinding glimpses of the obvious – which have contributed much to his leadership success. Frank Turner, MD of Lucas Aerospace, who as we saw earlier runs half-marathons, chooses scenic settings whenever possible, adding to the pleasure. His essential practice of taking along his dictaphone to capture fleeting ideas and insights is evidence of the creative times he has on these runs. Pleasure, relaxation, personal space – these all seem to add to our state of creativity. They cannot be separated from the 'work' of a leader, if we are to know the secrets of his success.

Michael Wemms at Tesco has notched up three London marathons, but along with more energetic pursuits like squash, adds roller skating and skateboarding to his repertoire of skills and interests. On the whole, squash, 'working out', and other more energetic pursuits were rarer among the leaders I interviewed, with an average age probably in the fifties. When undertaken, such energetic pursuits did not provide the beneficial thinking state that the less strenuous activities did. The conscious mind, it seems, was more concerned with the activity in hand, the pain it caused, or physical survival. The period of relaxation and relative exhilaration *after* the activity, however, was as prolific a thinking time as any. Wide and sometimes unusual sporting and hobby interests did, however, provide a rich set of acquaintances, with the different points of view they afforded.

Hothouse ideas in the garden

The garden is probably the number one contributor to British business success in the ideas it provokes at the highest level. Even those who were far from committed gardeners would link the conception of new ideas to the smell of mown grass (cut by somebody else), a quiet spot in the garden, or just being close to nature. Bob Nice, at Ratcliff Tail Lifts, has a literal 'hothouse' of ideas in his garden, a personal sanctuary of creativity where many of the company's successes over the years have been conceived. Sipko Huismans, chairman of Courtaulds, values the time it takes him to mow his oversize lawn. He recalls a major personal issue being resolved in a flash during one of these relaxing lawnmowing sessions. Paul Lester, MD of Graseby plc, has five hours of regular grasscutting that has become an important time for reflection and ideas. He can even associate special creativity with a certain part of the garden. Bob

Lawson, CE of Electrocomponents, gets most inspiration when digging.

Leaders on vacation

Answering the question, 'When did you find time for creative thinking as a cabinet minister?', Lord Young's instant answer was 'August'. This indicates the potential of a good holiday to get all kinds of business and personal matters in order, although perhaps is an indictment on the pressured way government and much business is conducted. A total change of environment, whether on holiday, on an overseas business trip, or attending a seminar or conference, seems to bring with it a welcome new perspective. On returning to the office, problems are not so insurmountable, and we see things in a clear and often better light. This is an area where successful leaders can pass on sound advice to workaholics, or any manager who has not yet distinguished inputs from outputs.

The reality is that there is not much you can do anyway if your mind decides it wants to think about business issues. It can be as futile to try to empty your mind of work when on holiday as willing yourself to go to sleep when your brain is determined to work late. So, although some leaders have more success than others in forgetting the business during a holiday, most I spoke to were no more in charge of their intuitive minds than during a normal weekend. Most plan to leave their corporate worries at the airport. Some, appreciating the creative opportunities of an extended relaxing period with plenty of personal space, were more than open to any gifts the creative mind cared to dispense. The more we relax and get into a pleasant state of mind, the more likely it is we will be at our most creative. And the chances are that the business, being high up in our overall personal ranking, will get the lion's share of that creativity.

Holidays are a particularly good time for solutions and ideas to emerge that have been consciously addressed earlier and which have been incubating – beneath our conscious thought – for some time. Different surroundings tend to evoke different perspectives, so eurekas are as likely to come while on holiday as at any time. And they can be worth weeks of hard grinding thought and activity in the benefits they bring. Fortunately, because they are such a vital survival mechanism, by very nature (like dreaming) doing what other modes of thinking cannot do, they can hardly be stopped once we are in a receptive state. We need to be either negligent in not recording and remembering the insight, or untrusting of their validity, if we are to completely negate this most sophisticated exhibition of human brainpower.

New ways to look at things

You don't have to wait for a Damascus road revelation. All kinds of opportunities on holiday might benefit the business, although some leaders, or perhaps their spouses, rule this out. One CEO, following an animated late night conversation over a game of chess with a fellow tourist, came back and radically changed his company's pension scheme, saving at least a fat consultancy fee and benefiting from a considerably improved scheme. Creativity is all about new ways of looking at things, and casual holiday meetings, involving people from different cultures and work backgrounds, can well supply the mental triggers that unlock good ideas. This is the leader taking yet another opportunity to keep in touch.

Derek Drake at Servowarm experienced plenty of mental creativity on a holiday in the isolated beauty of Ireland, cycling with his wife on a tandem. But the two or three super productive days immediately *after* the holiday attested to the real value of the mental and physical break. The time away was a wise investment, providing ideas and vitality to keep him going for a long time. Achieving and maintaining a balanced lifestyle is as valuable to the leader as any time management technique or entourage of PAs. Human Resources directors note, a real break from work now and again should be written into job descriptions. Top leaders seem to know this instinctively. Burned-out workaholics are no use to modern business.

Fortunately, we don't have to depend on holidays for our annual creativity. Any non-work time is an opportunity for creativity. Three o'clock in the morning was the modal time for memorable ideas that had an impact on the business, or for sheer ingenuity of thought – the sort of thinking that surprises the thinker. Travelling could be a therapeutic mental break and a source of moneyspinning ideas. Once away from the office and in leisure mode, just about any problem can be faced.

THE PLEASURE OF CREATIVITY

Another factor contributed to the overall 'leisure mode'. It was interesting that those executives who did *not* enjoy driving, but who tended to be stressed and very conscious of the actual journey, derived little thinking benefit. So as well as being linked to personal space, and a fairly relaxed state of mind, creativity is also related, it seems, to pleasure. Something as simple as washing the car, at least when perceived as pleasurable, can be enough to set the creative mind alight. Grant Rabey at RS Components enjoys his car-washing sessions, valuing the pleasure of the gleaming end product as therapeutic. The managing director of a leading national car dealer, who could avail himself of daily car valets if he so wished, reserves the weekly car wash to himself. The relaxation, sense of achievement and sheer pleasure he gets make this one of the most creative times in his week, producing a flow of ideas and solutions to problems. I met enough CEOs who loathe car washing and gardening to make it clear that if there is no pleasure in a 'leisure' activity, the mind is as sterile as when in the office at work.

Like work and leisure, the perception of pleasure and pain affects how we think intuitively. For many, washing the car – or gardening, or jogging, or driving – is *work*, and the mind seems to rebel against providing any kind of lateral thoughts in such a mode. This was confirmed over and over again as different activities – leisure for one, and work for another – produced very different levels of creative thought.

Vernon Sankey, CE of Reckitt and Colman, explains how he has his best ideas in the 'first few miles' of a jog. When the pleasure drops – literally when the pain is felt – all the creative thinking stops. Fellow jogger Jeffrey Herbert, at Charter plc, described how 'part of the time' he would be lost to his thoughts and come up with all kinds of useful ideas. He clearly had experienced the same phenomenon. So even a single run can swing from leisure to work, from pleasure to pain.

Recognising these varying states, and their effect on our clarity of thought and problem-solving, gives the leader an edge. Activities that evoke pleasure, especially if they are more or less unconsciously carried out as with driving, gardening or a sport, are a great occasion for solving corporate and other problems. The pleasure factor is another element in the pattern of leisure-mode thinking. It pays to build pleasurable occasions into your lifestyle, especially during what you now consider work time. Try to overcome the work ethic guilt, and recognise the real benefits to you and the business.

Occasionally, pleasure would go to high levels, as the

person was lost in either the beauty of nature or the sheer joy of being alone or simply – however inadequate the term – being 'at one with themselves'. Leaders who have developed a style of life that incorporates such times frequently – and this can be through music, art, any pastime, or just through the ability to turn off from immediate pressing circumstances – tend to be very creative and clear in their thought. I, and probably most of their followers, might describe them as 'outstanding'. Their creative thinking skills certainly explain much of their leadership success. Back at work, the pleasure in simply 'doing a job well' is clearly linked to the measurable results the job produces. We respond best when the rewards are inside – in fact, when what we are doing does not seem like work. This is an attitude to work that a manager can cultivate.

LEADING IN LIFESTYLE

One would have to struggle very hard to explain the special leadership ability we are discussing – or indeed any of the classical traits of leadership – in terms of genetics. Genetic factors, like intelligence (however it is defined and measured, in this context) are no doubt at work to some degree. But none of these factors is big enough to account for what gives leaders the special edge. Brains seem to come as standard, at least as hardware. The way we use the left side in education training, conventional problem-solving and analysis, and communicating in language results in a fairly predictable rise through business, or any other area of life. It produces plenty of managers, but precious few leaders.

The way we use the non-verbal right side is not nearly as clear. But what is clear from all the evidence is that, although the unconscious side of the brain does its clever things without our conscious intervention (so we don't have to be clever in the conventional sense, as is the case with highly gifted children or unschooled artists, writers or entrepreneurs) we have to give it time and space. In other words, we have to create the *environment* in which the right brain excels rather than is suppressed. And this, as we have seen, is more to do with lifestyle and personal values and beliefs than five-point formulas for management success, or conventional training. Any manager aspiring to leadership would do well to seek out this sort of lifestyle. Follow the tips at the end of the chapter.

The simple availability of the untapped potential of the brain opens up excellence to the millions who have hitherto closed their fuller minds by conforming to the treadmill of a blinkered, uncreative, me-too, left brain society. Lord Young was right; leaders are ordinary, just like scholars in the fifth form. They just use their mind and what resources they have in a way which makes the critical difference – that gives them the edge. Although our brain hardware is standard, what we do with this awesome resource, which in the case of the creative, intuitive right side of the brain does not rely on the trappings of western education and so-called intelligence (such as logical reasoning and verbal skills) is up to us. The software, if you like, is the self-awareness and the self-instruction. And this self-instruction can be of a strangely passive sort, such as when we 'think about something different' to enable us to 'incubate' a problem and come up with a solution later, without conscious effort. Not very professional or scientific, but supremely effective. Or the self-instruction to give yourself a bit of personal free-wheeling thinking space during which issues can be got into perspective and resolved in an optimal way rather than with the same old left brain logic that you and everybody else have been relying on.

The paradox is this: we seem to be at our most creative when in 'leisure' rather than 'work' mode. This is not true in every case, but does apply to most top people who are the product of formal education and training, and bureaucratic, structured employing organisations, and resulting career patterns. There is also the widespread vestige of the 'work ethic', which might explain the feelings of guilt at having fun when working; or even finding pleasure in work. The few publicised companies where work is said to be fun, where this mental distinction between work and leisure has been broken down, have shown just how powerful a change of attitude and culture can be for innovation. I did not delve any further into the massive hierarchies of the Times top 200 from which most of the leaders I interviewed were drawn, so I cannot say how many 'fun cultures' exist. I cannot imagine any of these large groups, the majority of which are bureaucracies, or at least are logically structured and heavily systems-based, making such a claim in any event. But wherever pockets of truly happy workers occur – and such cultures within cultures are well known – the result is always greater creativity and output.

The leader, having sorted out his or her own attitude to work and leisure, and having created personally the environment in which he or she is most fulfilled, becomes the prime model for a culture that encourages that same holistic view of the individual. Reassuringly, most of those I met genuinely wish for their companies to be a happy place to work, for all the people. The greater the trust and devolution of power, it seems, the greater is the real power of the leader – the collective power of followership rather than single leadership.

To act like a leader, as we saw in the last chapter, you have to think like a leader. We have now seen that in order to think like a leader, you have to live like a leader.

TIPS FOR TOMORROW'S LEADERS

1. Don't be a workaholic. That's not the way to the top – real leaders are smarter than that. Understand that any benefits from a work-only mentality are usually short-term.

2. Be creative at work, as far as your job permits. Check out with your boss how far you are able to come up with ideas or suggestions, both within your office or department, and concerning the company generally. Start creating your own creative environment.

3. Decide what place work and other interests take in your life, in terms of their priority. Make your mind up about any boundaries before you get sucked into situations you have not have planned for. Start being your own person.

4. Consider whether you are in the right job, and if not what you would prefer to be doing. You might not be able to change anything quickly, but you will establish a mental goal which will start to direct your unconscious mind to produce ideas. Expect some surprising insights into the choices you have, however impossible it might seem for things to change.

5. Seek to excel in everything you do, whether at work or away from work. One by one, drop the things you don't want to do, and have a go at things you have fancied doing. You can start by listing both categories in their order of importance to you.

6. Relax and wind down as frequently as possible. Think up ways for this to happen. Decide what you are going to do and when, and make any diary or other commitments you have to.

7. Decide you are going to have fun at work (even if it kills you) and see what difference your new attitude makes.

8. Make the most of any travelling time. Use it for quality thinking, including visualising forthcoming meetings, negotiations or other tasks as successfully achieved. Use any waiting or 'in-between' time in the same way.

9. Spend some time every day daydreaming. Imagine you are in some more senior position, and experience being the leader you are capable of being. Get to know what it feels like to lead.

10. Find time to be on your own with your thoughts every day. Get to know how you think. Practise remembering, being somebody different, achieving some new ambition, or changing your state of mind (e.g. become grateful, optimistic, thoughtful, confident, carefree, etc. at will).

11. Establish a favourite place, including a chair, where you can 'get away from it all'. Associate this place with particular creativity and ingenuity, and solutions to pressing problems. Respect and cultivate any places where you are more relaxed and can think easily.

12. Work out the time of day when you are at your creative best and make yourself more available – if need be, getting up a bit earlier, or getting away on your own at lunch time. Respect and cultivate your best thinking times.

6

Keeping in Touch

IN *In Search of Excellence*, Tom Peters and Robert Waterman talk about MBWA – management by wandering around (or walking about). They observed the practice in several 'excellent' American companies, and it was a major tenet of 'the HP [Hewlett Packard] way', then a model of corporate excellence. In the 1980s, informal communication throughout companies was identified widely as part of a formula for success. As it happens, several of Peters and Waterman's excellent corporations are no longer models of success. And in any case, MBWA was always more to do with personal leadership style than corporate communication. From the leader's point of view, it was all about keeping in touch.

Predictably enough, the practice tends to be favoured more by extroverts than introverts, and both types of personality fill positions of executive power. So the practice of MBWA is not a unique feature of top leadership. But the principle of *keeping in touch* is universally accepted by the leaders.

MANAGEMENT BY WALKING ABOUT

There are both manufacturing and service versions of MBWA. Manufacturers visit their plants, while retailers visit their stores. Sir Richard Greenbury, chairman of Marks & Spencer, visits a different store every Friday, confirming a tradition first established many years ago by the company's founders. Until he retired in 1984, Lord Sieff, Sir Richard's predecessor, was to be seen in the Marks & Spencer stores more than anywhere else. In this and many other cases, however, the practice has become institutionalised. Any retail store manager worth his or her salt, and most of the staff, will recognise their big bosses from the photographs displayed alongside the notice board or in the staff newspaper – so the surprise element is lost. It is doubtful whether these visits, which have become commonplace in the retail sector, have the same impact now as when they were first introduced by the earlier generation of entrepreneurial leaders, long before it was discovered and popularised by international management gurus.

On the other side of the counter

Some leaders are highly sceptical about the planned 'state visit'. Derek Williams at CCSB can get a lot from a debriefing, and feels the CE doesn't have to go everywhere. His style is informal and works best in an unstructured way. But one way or another, the leader has to avoid being confined to an ivory tower. Sir Rocco Forte, head of the Forte hotel group, commented 'Keeping track of the grass roots is an essential part of the way this company works.' This sentiment was repeated from one CEO to the next. Tom Vyner at Sainsbury's says there is 'no substitute for seeing, hearing, feeling and understanding – thinking like the customer . . . you need to get round to the other side of the counter.' He does his MBWA for real, turning up at four o'clock on a Saturday and making real purchases as a real customer. Richard Gooding, CE of London Luton Airport, has the advantage of a single site which he tours just about daily, as part of his natural open style. Archie Norman is just as visible in his Asda stores, and in his case is achieving a remarkably open culture, responding personally to literally thousands of suggestions from staff each year. He has made an effort to become a visible and accessible leader and the resulting culture is unmistakable. His business card reads 'Archie' and offers a 24-hour telephone number.

A lot of mega-retailers have their own brands of MBWA. Len Fyfe, now chairman of the Co-operative Wholesale Society, recalls a time when he would visit every one of his co-ops over the pre-Christmas period. Whilst this was of some value, it was the worst possible time of year for busy staff, and became impossible as the business grew. The 'Christmas blitz' has long since been replaced by frequent and more beneficial random visits throughout the year. The then Allied Breweries MD Douglas Strachan used to make a habit, when visiting depots, of walking up to the first person he saw and introducing himself. Some would be surprised, and even suspect a practical joke, but the internal PR value was high, and the leader kept in touch.

Early warning systems

The amount of information a boss can gather from a brief walk around a store is staggering. In his days at Sainsbury's, Peter Davis, until recently chairman of the publishing giant Reed International, would need no more than three or four minutes to get a feel for how a store was doing generally, and would spot enough in half an hour to keep the local manager occupied for weeks. John Hoerner, chief executive of the Burton Group (and also, as it happens, an ex-Sainsbury's man) is another veteran storewalker, who developed the same 'sixth sense' when visiting stores. It seems that the subconscious brain brings together all sorts of apparently insignificant details from a brief visit to make a lot of common sense. A few light bulbs that have not been replaced, sombre expressions on the faces of the staff, or averted eyes, some customers' remarks overheard, piped music too loud, hanging posters blocking the exit signs, and other 'signals' which on their own might have little meaning, together might indicate important problems with aspects of the management, staff attitudes, cost awareness and so on. Irene Graham at Target Life can instinctively tell if there is a backlog of work, or if staff are 'swinging lead'. These intuitive 'readings' when wandering around are important early warning signs which the best computer systems cannot replace. Rocco Forte says: 'I walk into an hotel and can see straight away how it is being kept. It makes me aware of problems long before they appear in the figures.'

Sometimes the benefits of a visit are not realised at the time. John Hoerner describes himself as a 'visualiser' and can recall each visit to a store in great detail – as if he were replaying a video recording. In his case the 'insights' often occur afterwards. Later the same evening, or the following day, he will 'play back' a visit, getting a flow of useful ideas which he quickly passes on to the appropriate staff (before he forgets), after which his short-term 'recording' seems to be erased for good. Other leaders I spoke to, without referring to such specific memory skills, nevertheless come up with ideas when least expected, but clearly triggered by a recent visit. All this is in addition to any observations made and discussed during a visit – usually of a more routine or predictable kind. There is usually a two-way benefit in MBWA. John Billing at Courtaulds Textiles represents many leaders when he says that he usually receives a lot more benefit than he gives on these visits.

More than experience at work

This sixth sense appears remarkable to those who are not familiar with it, although it is frequently put down simply to long experience by the leaders themselves. The construction industry has its own version of MBWA, the site visit. A construction site can be, for example, a large housing development, or a multi-million-pound overseas dam project. Like a large department store, such places offer a myriad messages to the acute observer. The trick here is to get a feel for how the project is doing in the three or four minutes Peter Davis would need to guess at the takings, margins, and staff morale of a retail outlet.

David Wilson heads up the Wilson Bowden construction and property group. On one visit to a large site he questioned a calculated work-in-progress figure, 'sensing' it was wildly overstated – even though the figure was based on detailed estimates by the best professionals. It turned out that his fears were justified – his almost instant judgement (the product, he insisted, of experience) was correct.

Equating intuition with long experience is common. The 'experience theory', however, quickly breaks down, as most of us know of colleagues with many years of experience whose judgement still cannot match that of a truly intuitive person. It is the way two people use the same experience that makes the crucial difference when it comes to leadership.

By the time I met Tony Palmer, CE of Taylor Woodrow, I had heard as many examples of such intuition from the cream of construction company leaders as from the retail bosses. The mud-caked bottom layers of brick stocks, or scaffold clips lying around on a site, and a hundred other signals to the subconscious, apparently act in the same way as blown light-bulbs or unreplaced stock in a retail setting. An obvious irregularity will be consciously spotted, and no doubt handled there and then. But most 'obvious' inefficiencies will already have been detected and corrected by good managers. So it is left to the extraordinary manager, or real leader, with an intuitive edge, to add something extra, and expose the mediocrity of conscious but blinkered thinking. MBWA is one way the leader can keep in touch using intuitive skills.

INTERPRETING 'PEOPLE SIGNALS'

Intuitive thinking is invaluable in any part of a business, and is readily transferable from company to company or industry to industry. It is intuition – rather than an MBA, or a first in economics – that has enabled 15-year-old apprentices to eventually find themselves chairing multi-billion pound groups. Formal academic qualifications, with their emphasis on conscious reasoning and analysis, are no match for powerful, holistic thinking.

Similar skills are used when dealing with people inside or outside the office. On one occasion Tony Palmer had the project manager of a very large overseas job in his office to give a progress report. One glance at the manager told him that things were not going well – something the project manager had hitherto done a good job of hiding from HO staff. In this case the true situation was revealed by the many subtle body language clues, clues that can give away the most poker-faced employee, customer or supplier. This skill in non-verbal communication, and a feel for the 'chemistry' between people, are other features of successful MBWA excursions, and part of what give top leaders the edge.

Peter Davis told me of an occasion when the 'people signals' turned out to be all-important. He and a regional director were visiting a Sainsbury's store in the company of the local manager, who, as it happened, had previously been assistant to the regional director in another store. As soon as

they walked into the shop, both Peter and his regional director knew something was wrong – both were familiar with
such intuitive but dependable feelings. Peter felt this was
specifically to do with the manager – rather than, as was
often the case, staff difficulties or logistics problems. He was
contradicted by the regional director, who, besides having a
lot of faith in his protégé, felt he would have been the first to
detect anything amiss. Taking the opportunity to get the
manager on one side on his own, Peter gently opened up a
discussion of the problem, at which the manager broke
down in tears. It transpired that he had been undergoing a
combination of domestic traumas, including a bereavement,
completely unbeknown to his staff and close friends.
Through some sort of sixth sense, Peter had uncovered the
problem, which could then be properly addressed. No obvious managerial skills would have picked this up, yet such
intuitive sensitivity might well be critical to the success of
this or any other business involving people. This demon-
strates the need for right brain skills to detect the signals
that identify a core problem or issue – and the important
edge such skills give a leader who is ready to watch and listen at the coal face of his business.

Rodney East at Etam describes how he has come to rely
on keeping in personal touch, however sophisticated the
reporting systems. A major store was redesigned quite radically, with lots of support and interest from the centre.
However, following one or two days of excellent results
(which usually are a reliable indicator of a successful
change) the sales plummeted. It might have been logical to
have abandoned the planned change and revert to what had
gone before, but Rodney 'knew instinctively' that there was
something wrong that none of the figures could reveal. On
this occasion he visited the store before it opened in the
morning, then proceeded to chat with the staff and manager
individually, only to discover there was very low morale, and

that the 'support' from head office had been counterproductive. The sales figures were more related to this staff attitude than to an otherwise successful redesign of the merchandising layout; allowing the local staff the initiative, recognising their unique contribution, was enough to turn around the whole situation. In this case, a potentially profitable marketing thrust might rationally have been abandoned, had not intuitive thinking and a reading of personal chemistry been part of Rodney East's leadership skills.

This extra sensitivity – a receptiveness to factors that might not fit experience to date or logic – is often absent in the case of financial, marketing or logistics managers who are focused functionally, and who have a strongly analytical training. Leaders, however, will not get far without this sensitivity.

Michael Wemms at Tesco makes lots of store visits and learns a lot from the assistants on the check-out tills. On a simple walk along the tills, he will tell by facial expressions and eye contact (or lack of contact) when things are wrong or staff are unhappy. He will take the opportunity to chat with a cashier not serving at the time, and the benefits turn out to be mutual – first-hand staff and customer feedback is received, whilst staff feel good and identify with the wider perspective of the leader. A good leader is sensitive to people, listening and observing even the tiniest signs. And much of this happens unconsciously.

MAKING OTHER PEOPLE'S IDEAS WORK

Stanley Kalms, chairman of Dixons, has been with the group since he was 16. For much of that period he has been at the helm, and he can be personally credited with a great deal of the group's success. Another creative thinker and inveterate storewalker, he, like many of his retail colleagues, is just as happy looking around somebody else's store as his own. (Unlike the secrecy which prevails in manufacturing industries, retailing is an open book.) It seems that, whatever the corporate communication case for MBWA in your own plant, site or stores, there is more mileage in getting outside familiar territory. An ideas man to the core, and almost frighteningly creative, Stanley does not credit himself with much original thinking – like most of his entrepreneurial contemporaries, he is happy to put it all down to experience.

On one visit to a northern store he noticed the difficulty bag-laden customers had in transporting small electrical goods – like kettles, electric curlers or toasters – to the check-out desk. When packed in boxes, these goods can be difficult to handle, along with other shopping. Like a flash the idea of trolleys came to his mind. Now there is nothing novel about trolleys, as a trip to any supermarket will confirm, but in this particular retailing context trolleys were an innovation, and a possible selling tool (particularly for the smaller-value items, where he had spotted there was a problem).

Stanley Kalms refers to himself as a 'mongrel innovator' – he combines other people's ideas and makes them work for him. And you don't get other people's ideas by staying in your own plant or shop. For the retailer, a walk down any high street can be an opportunity for mental data-gathering and new ideas. For example, Stanley noticed a familiar Casio watch display unit in a Ratner's jewellery store, prompting the idea that they should be introduced into Dixons – breaking the traditional monopoly of the jeweller's shop. All our senses come into play on these excursions. The bewitching smell of fresh bread in a competitor's store was enough to set Len Fyffe's mind working on the possibilities of 'piped' smell-power in the Co-op. There may be nothing new under the sun, but there are new ways of seeing things, and new ways of doing things in your own business.

Archie Norman at Asda visited the Nissan car plant in the north east of England for ideas. He also visits the US, in fact wherever companies have got a reputation for quality and customer care. On these visits he tries to ensure that he speaks with the workers themselves, and not just the bosses. These excursions are concerned with best practice, much of which is transferable from industry to commerce and vice versa. Len Simmonds and his managers, when running a newspaper group, have gone out to soft drinks, mining, transport, engineering, entertainment, and film-processing companies, as well as a school, a university, and other institutions, as part of their keeping in touch. The leader is primarily an example and enabler, and creates a culture in which the investment value of such visits is appreciated. Everybody in the business, and especially managers, must keep in touch.

THINKING LIKE THE CUSTOMER

The leader has to keep in touch with customers, as well as those inside the company. This often requires a whole new way of thinking, a different attitude. 'The moment you walk through the door, think like a customer – not a manager, check-out assistant or whatever' – the leader, as much as any marketing executive or salesperson, has to have this customer perspective. Sainsbury's and others use customer panels to gain detailed feedback about service. Michael Wemms at Tesco *becomes* a customer as frequently as possible – using the car park, filling up with petrol, using a credit card, or whatever – to know what it is like. David Quarmby at Sainsbury's makes a point of talking to at least three customers at every store he visits – usually choosing those with full trolleys, who are 'serious shoppers likely to have serious views'.

If you are a leader you have to be able to put yourself in somebody else's shoes, be they staff, customers, or suppliers. This is the crux of understanding the business. Bob Nice at Ratcliff Tail Lifts was brave enough to confront his top half-a-dozen customers and ask them exactly what they thought of the product, service, and the company. Although the exercise produced some alarming revelations, this particular version of keeping in touch resulted in major changes and benefits to the company. One customer's remark that he was 'sick of rust', for example, resulted in the development of a market-leading aluminium tail lift product range. Another customer had an unusual colour preference, but listening, plus some simple changes, soon brought welcome orders. Responding to the service needs of customers resulted in a highly profitable planned maintenance service. Customer service means keeping in touch, and the responsibility starts right at the top. This is all about thinking – the way the leader thinks, and the culture this creates – and especially about seeing things through the customer's eyes.

MBWA practice is significant for its variety, as it is carried out by very different leaders in very different businesses. Any technique has a tendency to work more for some than for others, and may not be readily transportable across company cultures. But it illustrates how some leaders keep in touch. And this, I found, was the more basic characteristic of the leader. The walking-around technique was always popular with more extrovert bosses, and those of Theory Y leaning. But, whatever the technique, keeping in touch is more than an optional extra for today's empowering leader.

THE DOWNSIDES OF MBWA

So what are the downsides of MBWA? Whilst just about every leader I interviewed has a personal place for it of some kind, at some level, there was plenty of scepticism about the standard hand-pressing version. Sir Anthony Gill, recently retired as chairman of Lucas, with a vast international business to serve, saw it as completely unrealistic to expect a single person to do justice to full shop-floor visits. The sheer scale of the business restricts the leader's ability to keep in touch with everything. Tesco, for example, might *open* 25 to 30 new stores each year. And many of our manufacturing groups, as well as retailers like Marks & Spencer, are scattered around the world. So a visit by the big boss from the other side of the world, in almost any corporate culture, will be of the state-visit kind. It can hardly be impromptu, and in terms of recognition and the feel-good effect on the part of the workers, it is likely that more contact with a closer level of management will be far more effective.

Sir Anthony Gill adopted a sampling approach, which allowed him to do reasonable justice to visits, while balancing his own time with other commitments of the leadership role. He also favoured making contact at a closer level in the hierarchy, going down say two tiers of management, again avoiding the state-visit danger, and looking for practical business benefits from any encounter. This approach was repeated in many other cases. Robert Lawson, CE of Electrocomponents, has a similarly wide spread of overseas plants. The first visit, he insists, is forced, and can hardly affect the level of trust or the culture that is the basis of real change. Even a 12,000-mile trip will find only one-third of the round-the-clock shifts waiting to enjoy the visit. And besides the geography, increasing automation in industrial

139

plants has dramatically reduced manpower. As Derek Williams puts it, at Coca-Cola Schweppes (CCSB), so much investment has gone into automation, with a handful of operators, that he is increasingly visiting machines.

In terms of the benefit of these encounters to the leader and the leader's role in the company – rather than pure staff relations – another factor is that outlets or plants tend to be very alike. This is especially the case with multiple retail outlets where, by design, there tends to be little deviation from highly centralised practice. In terms of providing new ideas to benefit the business, clone outlets are, by their nature, devoid of a variety of practices to generate new thinking. They can be positively mind-numbing by the three-hundredth walkabout.

As it happens, despite heavy centralisation, Marks & Spencer stores *can* have their own unique identity, sometimes based upon local managers' preferences, or a particular strength or tradition. One store, for instance, might be particularly strong on fish, and another on knitwear. The Kings Road store in Chelsea, London, for instance, has its own unique character reflecting its location and customers. The sheer scale of 650 stores worldwide, and their degree of individual character, gives Sir Richard Greenbury and Keith Oates a rich source of ideas – inside the company – that can be transferred from one branch to another.

Keeping things in perspective

Len Simmonds, then at T Bailey Forman, says the downside of MBWA is that you have to create an environment where it is done on such a regular basis that it becomes part of the norm, and the leader is 'accepted'. As we have seen, this can take many visits, and is not practical for the top leader in a large group. Another danger is that the leader, especially if promoted from within the business, will only go where he or she feels most comfortable – to an area where a discussion can be held about something. Leaders who have a genuine interest in people, and the intuitive skills to communicate even without technical knowledge of the work, have the edge and are likely to give and receive more from these visits.

Most of the leaders, besides expressing the value of getting outside their own office, felt that visits within the company were of value to the staff. A few, however, were sceptical, explaining how, for instance, circumventing normal lines of command could be counterproductive, as managers at different levels felt excluded, and this caused resentment. Many top leaders simply did not believe that comments from either managers or shop-floor workers were 'unfiltered'. To a large extent, it was felt, people – always with self-interest – amend their behaviour or what they say to suit the supervisor, manager, or big boss. In many cases the boss's visit is another occasion for personal or group welfare moans, or for political manoeuvring, or simply for conforming to the local management's well-communicated line.

One leader I spoke to was insistent on learning 'facts'. He discounted personal opinions and was wary of being told what people wanted him to hear, and of having his 'data-bank' distorted by politics and self-interest. So he was not a fan of MBWA, at least in his own company. Whilst this was an extreme view, it exemplifies an important truth about intuitive or right-brain thought: third-rate opinions will tend to produce third-rate ideas – trashy books will provide a source of trashy ideas. A shallow, narrow view of the world will produce very limited thinking. Tom Vyner at Sainsbury's is wisely cautious even about visualising, when the visualised imagery is based on outdated experience in a rapidly changing world. So the insightful leader has to open the windows of the mind to be as close as possible to the reality outside.

The value of keeping in touch

In a few cases the personality of the leader seemed to blur the real value of their visits as perceived by others. One chairman of a household-name retailer is seen by a competitor counterpart as evoking fear in store assistants whenever he makes a visit. It is not hard to imagine this being the case, even though the intention and perception of the leader in question is very different. In another case, regular visits by a chairman, considered by him to be highly valuable, evoke a reaction of anything from a troublesome intrusion to a joke. His tours are likely to be well orchestrated, and he is turned left and right as local occasion demands. A sense of worthwhile duty seems to have overtaken any original leadership purpose, and the result will almost certainly be counterproductive.

In other cases, however, and this is acknowledged by competitors, visits by the leader are looked forward to with pleasure, and result in all sorts of tangible benefits to the business. I noticed that in these (not too common) cases, and based on a reasonable consensus view across competing CEs, particularly in the retail sector, the leader was quite at home in the MBWA role, and seemed to enjoy the whole process. Moreover, the rapport had become part of the culture of the company, in some cases having been built up over quite a long leadership regime. Respect, and the privilege of genuinely unfiltered feedback, is earned by the leader; a valuing, empowering relationship it seems is not easily faked. Archie Norman at Asda has a style which, if emulated, would be unlikely to work in quite the way it does at Asda. 'But that's Archie' is the explanation for his success. And other far less visible leaders have helped create effective, empowering cultures by firstly being true to themselves, their beliefs and values.

OUT-OF-COMPANY EXPOSURE

The important thing is not to surround yourself with the familiar, which deadens creative thought. And this is where the benefit of out-of-company exposure is felt. Keeping in touch can be extended to visits to competitors having similar multiple outlets or plants. McDonald's, the epitome of retail cloning and standardisation, are an object lesson in their sort of business; as recounted earlier, Rodney East dates several initiatives at Etam back to a forced encounter with one of their restaurants in central Milton Keynes, when he had lost his car keys. But the law of diminishing returns applies in a classic way to such visits. Tony Wilkinson, chairman of the Wilkinson group, although himself running a chain, does not visit chains for his inspiration other than in the course of normal shopping, which, as a real customer, continues to provide important insights. Instead he visits local one-off retailers, some of which achieve a level of excellence that the multiples could well learn from. A specialist chocolate shop got five-star rating, and provided evidence of a level of customer care that large organisations struggle to achieve. And this was in one local high street wander. For Tony, book shops and wine shops are most likely to fuel his creative mind, reflecting his own interests.

These are retail examples, but only a blinkered left brain approach would fail to make the connections between very different retail businesses, or between manufacturing and service operations. Customer service is expressed in a language that readily crosses business barriers – quality is quality in any business, and the same principles apply. A Formula One racing car pit, or a corner-shop stock system, can be as instructive as any big plant process. So leaders have learned to add value in their roles, by keeping in touch effectively, allowing their senses to be bombarded by anything that is new or that might stimulate new perspectives and creative insight.

Nuclear Electric, in bringing about far-reaching changes in the company, visited scores of companies in a wide range of sectors, to learn what they could from both successes and failures. At first they thought they were unique in the way they operated, but soon realised that there were more similarities than differences between themselves and other companies. At the same time they began to be discontent with the standards they had achieved hitherto, so visits took on bench-marking signficance. But Robert Hawley stresses that as many people as possible must be involved in this process. It's no good just sending managers on visits, even if they come back proclaiming they have seen the light – staff might still be in the dark. So a cross section of managers, staff, and trade union representatives were involved in the visits. To avoid the activity being seen as 'corporate tourism', the teams involved presented what they had learned to other staff soon after getting back to the company. Nuclear Electric report major benefit from their outward-looking policy.

CROSSING CULTURAL BOUNDARIES

The leader is able to see things from different points of view, and thus has more choices upon which to base judgements and decisions. A real understanding of the market, for example, comes not just from numbers and analysis, but by imagining successfully what the customer thinks and feels – putting yourself into his or her shoes. To get the best out of staff, the leader has to have empathy, an understanding of how people think and feel; no organisation structure or rewards system will replace this basic requirement, which is at the heart of empowerment and leadership. Hence the importance of keeping in touch, both within and outside the organisation. But the biggest benefits are gained when new and different perspectives are welcomed, even though these might be disturbing to the status quo, and might contradict the way we have always done things. Such insights usually came from outside the familiar boundaries of the organisation and indeed the industry, and, in a non-work context, outside the familiar boundary of existing interests and social circle. The leader has to get *outside* his or her own culture, in its broadest sense.

Doing this can range from contact with shop floor and junior administration workers – rather than just with managers – inside the company, to a wide social life outside, providing different ideas and viewpoints, and exposure to cultures in other societies. John Conlan at First Leisure insists you have got to get away from 'the trappings of business'. Richard Sykes at Glaxo reckons that 90 per cent of his ideas come from outside of business. Crossing cultural boundaries, or getting outside your comfortable way of seeing the world, is part of leadership.

A global vision

The international dimension is critical because of the increasing globalisation of products and markets. Leaders have to exercise the vision that can encompass the opportunities of worldwide information technology. But from a thinking point of view, crossing national, racial and religious cultures has its own benefits which are less appreciated. Insight into how, say, the Japanese might perceive an issue such as decision-making, control, quality, value or motivation, might be of greater benefit than hard technological information.

In principle this 'seeing into the other person's mind' is no different to understanding how your own production worker or ledger clerk perceives something. But because of the greater cultural gap in another industry or country, the difference is usually more jolting to our comfortable way of seeing things. Given a perspective that might be totally different from our own, there is less danger of what we hear and see being pigeonholed along with existing mindsets, to reinforce them further.

Sometimes we need a whack on the head before we really see things the way the other person does. Today's leader, more than ever, has to think cross-culturally. And this does not just relate to ever-opening markets and world products – customers and suppliers have different requirements which have to be differentiated – but because a leader has to draw personal ideas, insights and inspiration from as wide and rich a source as possible.

Overseas store-wandering

The MBWA examples showed how much more benefit can be got from wandering around a competitor's store or plant than your own, especially if you have been in the same business for some years. Better ideas, certainly in quality rather than quantity, can be got by wandering even further afield: for winning ideas you may need to venture well beyond the local high street. Grahame Winter, formerly group managing director of Allied Maples, recently bought out the Maples furniture chain (in itself an outstanding story of enterprise). He has taken to wandering around American shopping malls to get his business inspiration. Armed with a notepad, a childlike curiosity and a willingness to learn, he looks and listens, and returns to his UK company with scores of useful, profitable ideas. Grahame introduced a radical new warranty policy in the Allied Maples group after overhearing a chance conversation between an American customer and a shop assistant. The strangeness of the environment and sometimes the very different ways of thinking from country to country, seem to make us more receptive to ideas.

Prior to introducing the highly successful Marks & Spencer chargecard and developing their financial services business, Keith Oates, joint managing director when we met (he is now deputy chairman and describes himself as a 'new boy', having had only ten years with the company!), also availed himself of a US trip. This included a visit to the world-famous Sears Roebuck department stores. Sears had recently acquired two new businesses in real estate and stock-broking, to add to a long-held insurance company. These were represented by three desks near the store entrance. Being interested in a similar diversification at Marks & Spencer, Keith made some enquiries at the desks about how each business worked together (as in cross-referring leads) and asked about other benefits from the mergers. To his surprise he learned that, despite the physical proximity of the desks, there was little or no communication between the new businesses, or between them and the parent company Sears.

The insight he brought back from his overseas store-wandering was how *not* to introduce the new financial services business into Marks & Spencer. Rather, his strategy would be to introduce the services organically, through internal change and growth. His judgement, based on keeping in touch and crossing cultural boundaries, and finding an approach which felt intuitively 'right', turned out to be a winner for Marks & Spencer. Chargecard holders now total four million, and the financial services part of the business has become a major contributor to the group's profits, growing at a rate of 40 per cent year on year for the last four years. Keith's judgement was doubly confirmed when, just a few years after his US visit, Sears decided to divest themselves of most of those acquisitions.

The same US trip provided another eye-opener for Keith Oates. He was disturbed to find a major part of Marks & Spencer's investment in information technology lagged behind that in many US retail stores, and that this trend was likely to follow in Europe. This eventually triggered major changes at the tills and elsewhere, which put the group firmly among the leaders in the UK, where they have since stayed.

Keith never ceases to look for ideas. In a South of France supermarket five years ago he encountered a device for packing customers' plastic carrier bags, consisting of two wires along which the open bag slid, to be duly delivered full at the end of the check-out by the time the customer's change was handed over. He immediately set out to explore what could be done to meet an obvious customer need (already being addressed by M&S in the form of extra assistants to help customers pack their bags). With their considerable resources, M&S might well come up with a solution that is far superior to the French one. Another idea he picked up was a display of a cut-away suit, exposing the lining and manufacturing technique, which was on display at one of M&S's own stores in Barcelona. Like Stanley Kalms at Dixons, Keith Oates is happy to borrow ideas from outside his own company and country. Even as close as the Isle of Wight, there is a cultural difference that can lend itself to insights. It came as a revelation to Keith that some M&S customers on the Isle of Wight seemed unaware of the main customer policies of the store, such as exchanging goods. Reflecting on the fact, he then learned that 40 per cent of the residents of the island have never visited mainland Britain. It all 'made sense' and appropriate measures could then be taken to communicate what are valuable selling features. But, when crossing cultures, overcoming physical distance is not nearly as important as having an open mental attitude, and thinking like the customer – wherever he or she happens to be.

STAYING OPEN TO NEW IDEAS

Mike Jackson got some inspiration for his building society from a visit to the USA, where he found the staff of a carpet firm had personally signed their customer charter. Mike took the idea and built on it, creating an impressive window display complete with large photographs as well as signatures to emphasise the staff's commitment to their customer charter. Whilst representing nothing new in theory, the intuition, based on the real sights, sounds, smells and feelings in another culture, brought about the important decisiveness.

All this happens outside the corporate office, and can be as valuable as any market research, especially if the leader's openness to new ideas is reflected in his team and staff generally. The would-be business leader has to have an openness to new ideas that draws on wide, everyday experience, however unfamiliar and irrelevant it may seem, to help achieve goals. There also has to be a simple trust in the ideas and insights the mind offers, often by the subtlest of associations. A mind that is confined to sequential logic and analysis, or received wisdom, as the basis for innovation will not share in the successes of these wandering leaders.

Leaders of companies operating internationally have more opportunity than most to reap the benefits of experiencing different overseas cultures. Sainsbury's were able to learn a lot from their US businesses in the area of electronic point of sale scanning, now an everyday part of the European retail scene. Although the technology was widely known at the time, practical experience in the US proved invaluable and helped to give Sainsbury's a head-start in pioneering the technique in the UK.

Sipko Huismans, chairman of Courtaulds, as it happened, was a long way from his home base when a memorable idea struck him. Walking down a crowded street in Singapore, the sheer size of the Far East market dawned on him. He resolved there and then to appoint a director to the board with specific responsibility for that region. Nothing outwardly changed – he was the same person walking down the same street – but the impact of the experience was unmistakable. And because these intuitive thoughts tend to be holistic – looking at things from many different viewpoints – the idea included also who the director would be. Two or three, or ten, different issues or problems – human resources, technological, financial – can be 'solved' in one moment of insight. Even though you may be well aware of a market and its potential, in theory – as Sipko Huisman was – it often takes the heart as well as the mind to goad you into action.

Wherever you are, your mental receptiveness is what counts. Perceptions can be just as blinkered in a foreign plant or village market as when you are walking through your own familiar office corridors. Some of the leaders I spoke to introduced some discipline into overseas trips by requiring of themselves a number of good, usable ideas to bring back. You can't manufacture eurekas, but you can get away from what is familiar; you can start to watch and listen, and induce an expectancy for solutions.

EXPOSURE TO DIFFERENT VIEWPOINTS

We are less likely to cross cultures by staying within the normal routine of work and leisure life. There is the danger of living in a world of business and business people, with no exposure to 'ordinary' people. A few of the leaders I met like to mix with artists and others who have a very different outlook to that of the average businessman or professional manager. Some choose not to socialise much with work people, valuing the richness of a wide and different sort of leisure time acquaintance. This is another dimension of keeping in touch. It is helped, of course, by a diversity of non-work interests, hobbies and pastimes which bring the leader into contact with all sorts of people. But this wide social interaction only becomes significant if it provides a source of intuitive and innovative thinking. At the time I met Len Simmonds, then MD of T Bailey Forman, he had a forthcoming meeting with a bishop and was determined to get some positive benefit from his exposure to a different viewpoint. But the opportunity itself had arisen because of an ongoing interest outside his immediate job that allowed wider cultural relationships.

For the busy executive, such interests may have to be fostered, with the longer-term aim of better thinking – gaining an important edge – or they may never happen. Tony Wilkinson is involved with a village green committee. A problem the committee faced, to do with getting rid of weeds on the green, raised the question of the availability of the necessary weedkiller, which, despite its potentially very harmful effects, was readily available in Tony's and other stores, but with legal requirements as to its use. This led Wilkinsons to do a check on how this sort of product was controlled, and the liabilities it involved. Following highly publicised illegal disposal by big retailers of similar products flushed down lavatories, the review was timely, although something that might well have been left to the very bottom of any priority listing. And it started with weeds on the village green. This is not to say that there needs to be any direct link, or benefit, from any out-of-work involvement. Such a link is probably the exception rather than the rule. Rather it is the general widening of perspective, and the fertile mind this creates – better thinking – that will inevitably produce winning ideas for the business.

Outside interests

Many of the top leaders I met had other business as well as social and personal interests. Non-executive directorships, typically with companies in completely different industries, bring benefits to the intuitive leader far greater than is apparent. The novelty of how things are done somewhere else tends to trigger far more ideas than what goes on in your own board room. Stanley Kalms joined the board of British Gas and after one meeting 'borrowed' their board structure and applied it to Dixons. Sir Denys Henderson, chairman of ICI and Zeneca, also values his involvement with other boards. Sir Anthony Cleaver, former chairman of IBM UK sees outside interests as having a major effect on the business. Whether these outside interests are business or social is not as important as whether the interest is different to your main work, and offers new perspectives on what you do. Small company exposure is important to a big company chairman – and vice versa. Many business leaders are involved in hospital trusts, schools, academic institutions, training and enterprise councils, and a whole range of public and charitable organisations.

All this makes for a wider and richer context for thinking and decision-making. As we have seen, international and cross-cultural exposure can also help creativity and innovation. And the relaxed, pleasurable state of leisure – although differing from person to person – seems to add a further dimension of creative power. These are some of the patterns of successful leadership.

A WAY OF THINKING

Thinking creatively and seeing things from new perspectives is a way of thinking – an attitude. You don't necessarily get rich, innovative thoughts by travelling the world, any more than by doing a tour of your regional offices. Given an open, receptive, listening attitude, however, the further away you get from what is familiar and routine, the better for creative thought. But the mind can be opened by reading a good book, by a casual conversation with a stranger, or by taking part in some activity outside the normal confines of your business.

The leaders I met engage in a wide variety of non-business activities and interests. There are also some obsessive readers among the ranks of British business leaders – Jim Smith at Eastern Electricity, for intstance, has set himself a ten-year reading programme, during which he will cover what he thinks is the best in English literature. Sir Neil Shaw, chairman of Tate and Lyle, and Tony Wilkinson, chairman of the Wilkinson group, are also 'voracious' readers. This is another way to cross cultures – *mentally* – another source for the mental databank upon which quality intuition draws; another way for the leader to keep in touch.

TIPS FOR TOMORROW'S LEADERS

1. Keep in touch with your staff and the business. Go to places where you are not familiar with the people, functions, or products – don't confine yourself to your own staff or department.

2. Set simple objectives for any walkabout. For example, speak to so many people, or come back with so many ideas, such as for saving costs or a quality improvement. Or perhaps decide to offer praise to somebody.

3. Have an overall 'keeping in touch' strategy. Give it due place in your diary. Be careful you don't step on any toes when straying outside your area of responsibility.

4. Watch and listen more than you talk. Always be courteous and show that you want to learn rather than teach. Keep any promises you make.

5. Be open to unconscious 'signals'. See more than the obvious. Reflect on a visit afterwards, as ideas might occur to you later.

6. Pretend you are a customer or client – live the role now and again. Think like a customer, and see what insights that brings.

7. Consider what you need to know on a regular basis to keep in touch with all aspects of your work. Write down what you have to *do*, and commit and plan accordingly.

8. Get out to see how your main competitors do things. Copy whatever you can, but try and use your creative powers to be better.

9. Get as far away as possible from your own business to get different perspectives. You can do this by extending your out-of-work interests, as well as by visiting competitors' plants, meeting people at conferences, or whatever.

10. Put yourself in the shoes of someone with a very different cultural view of things. For example, imagine you are a round-the-world sailor, or a travelling circus artist. Use the imagination you had as a child. Have a new look at your familiar surroundings and acquaintances through different eyes.

11. Meet different kinds of people who are likely to have different opinions about things. Get right outside your social group from time to time, and be prepared to listen.

12. Make associations between work and social and domestic situations. Expect ideas to come from anywhere.

13. Take an interest in what others do – especially if you cannot 'see yourself' doing what they do.

14. Make time for reading. Keep abreast of your business in any way possible, even if through second-hand sources. But be selective in how you keep in touch – you can't read everything, visit everywhere, or speak to everyone. As a rule, go for quality.

7

Choosing and Empowering People

BEING ABLE TO CHOOSE the best people is a crucial aspect of good leadership – this was confirmed again and again in my discussions with those at the top. The whole process of recruitment is highly sophisticated and professional. With the development of assessment centres, psychometric testing, and a whole range of techniques for better selection, there is no shortage of ideas and information on the subject.

The leader, as it happens, is spared much of the initial processing in recruitment, although some take a particular interest in one or more aspects. One chairman of a household name group, for instance, is heavily into graphology, the art of inferring a person's character from their handwriting. Another pursues a theory about prominent eyebrows. Some like pressure interviews, probing what might be vulnerable areas, whilst others stress the importance of meeting spouses. But most have a healthy scepticism of straying too far from face-to-face interviews. Although some interesting interviewing techniques were divulged, these were far from representative of what most of these leaders did. Nor did they illustrate the distinctive nature of leadership. The common feature was much more basic, and concerned the importance of judgement, intuition, and the subtle

156

interpersonal skills, including personal 'chemistry', involved in dealing with people generally.

This is an area where right brain skills come into their own. People are largely unpredictable and irrational – at least in the eye of the beholder who considers himself rational. It seems that the best organisation structures and watertight systems are there just to be misused or ignored by otherwise reasonable people. Customers don't do what we want or expect them to, and staff are no more considerate. So we have to call on special powers to choose those we want to work for us, or in whom we need to place trust. This is where the idea of personal chemistry keeps cropping up – the intuitive 'feeling' about a person that makes us like or dislike them. Although different words were used, the concept of personal chemistry was universally understood by the leaders we talked to. What differed was the degree to which they felt themselves adept at the instinctive process of judging people (whilst probably recognising and appreciating it in others, such as their wives), and the extent to which they trusted and acted upon their instincts.

CHOOSING KEY PEOPLE

Leadership is about followership. The choice of key people probably tips the balance in any ranking of successful leadership criteria. So how does this happen, and what sets the true leader apart from the average manager or even professional recruitment manager? The real test is in recruiting staff from outside the company, where there is no long experience of working together, or reliable opinion to be sought from other trusted staff.

The common practice of internal recruitment partly helps to minimise the risks. But the downside of such a policy, perhaps in perpetuating a less than ideal culture and reducing fresh thinking, is obvious. 'People decisions', whether they involve staff, customers, suppliers, bankers, or whoever, are central to business and to leaders in particular, and you do not always have the advantage of a prior relationship.

In the case of recruitment from outside, opinions are formed, of course, during a reading of the CV and any supporting comments, but these – however time-consuming they may be – can be quickly outweighed by the impact of the first face-to-face meeting. What happens during the job interview process, including first impressions, can give clues as to the way leaders interact with others, and the way this interaction affects decisions, and eventual company performance. The consequences of a senior appointment are likely to be far-reaching, and are bound to affect the success of the incumbent leader. So he needs to get a high percentage of important 'people decisions' right.

Judgement and personal 'chemistry'

Chief executives of the big groups have one thing in common – a human resources function which does a professional job of recruitment, and spares them anything other than the final stages of the process. In some cases extensive psychometric testing and/or assessment centres are used (although many of the top managers I met were most articulate in their scepticism of some such devices), and there is usually recourse to outside specialists somewhere in the process. The result of all this is not to *make* a decision, but to *require* a decision – a choice between a final shortlist of acceptable candidates. And this is where the leader comes in, at least for higher-level posts, and particularly those where there will be some personal contact between the leader and the person being hired.

All the logical processes and systems fail to make the final decision. The chief executive might well have the knowledge to add a further logical tier of appraisal, especially if his or her own experience and field of expertise happens to overlap. But the leader is likely to be far more concerned with the character and personal qualities of the candidate, and whether he or she will fit the company culture, than checking on the detailed CV. What is called for, more often than not, is simple judgement – based not just upon the experience, qualifications and track record of the candidate, all of which have been checked out by professionals, but on some intuitive faculty that does not seem to be based on logic at all.

There are wide differences between leaders as to what personal chemistry is all about. Very few doubt its importance, and a good majority rank it higher than all the selection and vetting procedures put together. Robert Ayling, chief executive of British Airways, appropriately refers to his 'radar system'. Sir Nicholas Goodison, chairman of the TSB group, talks about a 'nose' for people. And Fiona Colquhorn, the human resources boss at Cable and Wireless, refers to an 'electrical connection'. Robert Sykes at Glaxo uses a common expression when he says 'I warmed toward him.' Stanley Kalms reckons he is getting to know the 'personal agenda' of the person, and Derek Williams at CCSB asks 'Has he got the same agenda?' Many others spoke openly of a simple like or dislike.

Making a quick impression

But one aspect of this 'chemistry' applies universally – the speed with which this initial, instinctive judgement is made. Even those who were sceptical of the value of a quick impression, and who tended to react against it in the later stages of an interview – some even feeling guilty that they could think in such an irrational way – acknowledged the awesome speed of the intuitive process. So within a matter of a few minutes at the outside, and more typically 'seconds' or 'instantly', a first and very important impression is made.

Stanley Kalms, the Dixons' chief, John Conlan at First Leisure, John Hoerner of the Burton Group, Peter Ellwood, group chief executive of TSB, Sir Robert Evans, formerly at British Gas, and many others have described this very real phenomenon and its speed. 'Instantaneous like or dislike', and 'massive reliance on intuition' are the sort of expressions used. Bronwyn Curtis at Letherby and Christopher used the phrase in one description, which is probably the most common: 'As soon as he walked through the door . . .'. Intuition about people is often as fast as that. David Lyon, CE at Bowater, refers to 'three seconds' or 'when walking to the lift'. There is no time for left brain analysis, in which the many detailed characteristics – the *parts* – of the person are considered. It is a different kind of thinking. The *whole* person is seen – or the many parts are viewed *in parallel*. By its very nature, this holistic way of thinking, however annoying it is in its lack of an ordinary logical basis, is uncannily quick in its operation.

Trusting your people judgement

The list of those business leaders with a high-speed sixth sense for judging people is both long and impressive. And wherever all this fits into management science, it is high on the agenda of the leaders. So how dependable is this sometimes uninvited kind of thinking? There was an interesting paradox in what the chief executives and chairmen had to say. In several cases there was scepticism and even guilt at forming instant opinions. Frequently these first impressions had to be consciously suppressed, in case they clouded judgement during the remainder of an interview, or they were objectively treated as some kind of prejudice – an aberration of the logical, rational thinking of the professional manager. But then I put the question: does this early 'chemistry' have any effect on a final decision? And the answer was a resounding positive. Indeed it was more typical that, in the case of positive chemistry, a candidate unknowingly won an instant ally, willing him or her to succeed; and that in the case of a negative reaction, the poor candidate had to climb out of a deep hole.

Beyond the interview, on later reflection, perhaps after discussion with colleagues and at the time of the actual decision, the instinctive feeling, based on the initial moments of the meeting, had a disproportionately strong effect – far greater, for example, than experience and qualifications, references taken up, or the results of a psychometric test. It was a nagging, prompting memory of the 'feeling' the thought of the person evoked. In some cases, where the leader had come to trust these feelings (usually over a number of years), the chemistry might result in the boss overriding several colleagues, and a decision might certainly go counter to the indications of a curriculum vitae and established track record. In short, he has *learned*, usually by bitter experience, to trust his feelings.

Denis Stoyles, managing director of Butteknit, a small fashion clothing company, cancelled some 20 remaining interviews for the post of finance director, being intuitively sure about a particular candidate, even though the person had the worst CV of the lot. Unsure of just why there was this mismatch between feelings and the unassailable facts of the CV and 'scientific' tests, a telling quote was, 'I usually get it right for the wrong reasons.' One way or another, personal chemistry, however instant, intangible or illogical, is an overriding factor in the recruitment decision.

Hit rates in choosing winners

But the paradox goes even further. Asked how those initial impressions turned out with hindsight – whether they were proven to be reliable over the longer term – the standard response was something like: 'I can count on one hand the number of times my initial instinct [feelings, reaction, chemistry – whatever] has let me down.' Sir John Hoskyns, chairman of Burtons, is 'seldom completely wrong'. Sipko Huismans at Courtaulds is 'almost always right' – and, like many, he times the whole process in seconds. When hit rates were quoted they were over the 90 per cent mark. Having appointed his finance director, Denis Stoyles would have long arguments with him, as he was a solid, left brain analytical thinker and could not come to terms with Denis's hunches and unsupported decisions. As the months went by, however, the FD conceded a success rate of over 80 per cent, and from that point the mutual respect and partnership grew.

This reliance on quick impressions raises (at least in my sceptical mind) the likelihood of self-fulfilling prophecies. So I was somewhat surprised at how ready these business leaders were to relate, not their successes, but their failures – the times when they had got it memorably wrong. At this high level such failures turned out to be very expensive and well publicised in any case. What also stuck in the memory of the CEO or chairman were the times when they had got it wrong in another way – by ignoring or going against early chemistry in the cold light of later conscious thought and discussion. First impressions were suppressed or ignored. As Sir Ralph Robins, chairman of Rolls-Royce, succinctly put it: 'judgement right, decision wrong'. In such cases – but perhaps not until an expensive failure has occurred as a result of a senior appointment – the memory is associated back to a fleeting, but nonetheless real first impression which should have been a warning.

In this sort of case, which repeated itself over and over in our discussions, the quality of the subconscious, holistic 'reading' of another person turned out to be of the highest order – not infallible, but far more reliable than any system or technique. Bryan Drake, now MD of Servowarm, once had 'misgivings' about a candidate, but was under some pressure to make a quick appointment. At a second interview the candidate came across much better and Bryan rationalised away his initial doubts. Within a few months, however, the appointment was seen to be an unmistakable disaster and the post was terminated, with the usual animosity and cost to the company.

Choosing between heart and head

There is something unique about the very first, truly intuitive reaction to a person. It is often a subtle 'sensation' and might be suppressed, or not even consciously registered at the time. Later, however, the memory might be triggered by a negative 'warning' that went undetected by the conscious mind – perhaps a passing comment that seemed incongruent at the time and was overtaken and forgotten. But in the case of experienced and highly successful leaders – who are where they are largely through people skills – this personal chemistry is a well known phenomenon. At worst, it ranked equally alongside all the other more comprehensible data as a factor in a recruitment decision. For those leaders who had this particular right brain gift in good measure, it was high up on their list of leadership success factors.

None of this is to undermine the importance of CVs, references, or psychometric testing generally, although there were wide differences of opinion about their respective value. And we certainly cannot dispense with the interview process *per se*, including successive meetings involving different company people. Leslie Hill at Central Television and one or two others stressed this. But many of these functions are delegated to professionals in any event, and few top leaders could do justice to involvement in more than final interviews. As we saw earlier, such processes can produce a viable shortlist of candidates, but rarely a final decision. This is where the leader comes in. And this is where another perspective, at worst, is called for. In the case of the best judges of human character – where the leader's skill has to be focused – it is the intuitive sixth sense. Intuition is not the only factor, but in the case of top leaders it is a big one.

There is no shortage of anecdotal evidence of the power and reliability of intuition, especially when it comes to decisions about people. Jeffrey Herbert, CE of Charter plc 'did not like' a candidate for a key US appointment, although the other two members of the top US team were in favour of the appointment, and argued their case strongly. The appointment went ahead on the basis of all the logical evidence, only to prove disastrous and costly, the new director lasting about 18 months in the post. Anecdotes like this were repeated scores of times. Marks & Spencer recognised the particular skill of one of their senior people in spotting winners (and losers) consistently, even though he was not qualified to make an appraisal on any technical or business basis. He was brought into important interviews for the sole purpose of expressing an intuition; his track record of success, based on long hindsight, was remarkable, and he continued his specialised role until his recent retirement. So even if a leader does not have highly developed people skills, he or she needs to have an appreciation of the intuitive skills of others.

Prejudice or premonition?

It is important not to confuse this phenomenon with other factors involved in personal relationships. A lot of the leaders were more than aware of the danger of sheer prejudice. Some confessed openly to having an aversion to fat people, beards, ginger hair, certain accents, staring eyes, as well as the colour of suits, socks and ties (in this case the chairmen and chief executives will enjoy anonymity), and all manner of idiosyncrasies that probably revealed more about the interviewer than the interviewee. A retailing magnate summarily turned down one male candidate who was 'far too pretty'! Another case, also in retailing, involved a coloured jumper (but, to be fair, the candidate also refused to work on Saturdays).

Although some of our prejudices remain well below our consciousness, in these cases they were well known, and allowed for. And here is the fascinating aspect of real 'chemistry'; it sometimes overrides the known factors that might influence a decision irrationally – you can like a person without really knowing why, and despite conscious signals to the contrary. If the deeper chemistry is right, a ginger hair prejudice is no longer an issue. And the intuitive early impressions that turn out to be the best, sometimes only after several years, are those that come right from the subconscious – the genuine messages from the right-brain.

So if people are really vital to a leader's success, and their choice is so influenced by these little understood right brain thought processes, we have a further clue about what makes the important leadership difference. This is yet another aspect of intuition and judgement at work in interpersonal relationships.

Matching culture and values

An interview is often extended and probing so that the leader can bring to bear all his or her experience from the company and industry, as well as of people generally – and all this, on the face of it, is a *logical* process of questioning and feedback. But more is happening. Typically the main tests are whether a person will 'fit' in the actual job, and whether he or she will fit in the company, with its perhaps distinctive culture. This is more than a personal like or dis-like, but a role and culture matching. David Lyon at Bowater asks: 'Will he fit the role?' It might extend also to beliefs and values. Sir David Alliance, chairman of Coats Viyella, for instance, might enquire about when the candidate last visited his or her parents. He holds family and other values as important, and these will affect his decision. Different values might be important to another leader, and the line of questioning will seek to elicit answers which support the value 'test'. In any event, further judgement of some sort is needed – more intuition rather than logic – not least, regarding the honesty of what is said. So the right brain is not confined to the first impression. Intuitive skills pervade all interpersonal dealings.

Interestingly, it seems that the chemistry process might be a sophisticated mechanism which is able (from body language, eye contact, tone of voice, and hundreds of rapid sensual readings) to elicit core values, such as integrity, and valuing of people, based upon a lifetime of stored memories of people who meet these core value criteria. So a *cloning* of sorts occurs, in which values – as distinct from personality traits or other more externally recognisable factors – are matched. In this way 'liking' means 'you are like me', in the important area of values, rather than, for example, in extroversion or introversion, accent or educational background. These core values tend to be few, and centre around integrity and respect for others. But such values are paramount (although perhaps unconsciously) for the leader, and come out in this 'chemical' testing.

These values come out in the leader's descriptions of what they are looking for in an interview candidate. As well as looking for someone who has respect for the individual, humility, and is able to see 'the big picture', Peter Ellwood at TSB looks for someone who will challenge him. The importance of this strong challenging personality was also echoed by Jack Rowell, manager of the England rugby union squad, and Bob Ayling, CE of British Airways. This reflects another leadership quality of seeking people who are better than you are, rather than someone who will not pose a career threat, or a yes-man. Sir Anthony Cleaver, former chairman of IBM UK, added openness, and a bit of deviousness, to his own list of desired personality traits. Some look for a very positive approach. As Robert Hoerner put it, leadership is about what we *should* do, not what we *shouldn't* do. Perhaps unknowingly, in describing their ideal appointees (challenging, good sense of humour, willing to break the rules, enthusiastic, etc) they were describing themselves, and thus supporting the 'values cloning' idea.

The almost universal instant chemistry we have seen uncannily detects these strongly held values – rather than more visible personality characteristics such as extroversion or introversion – so the leader has an unconscious filter which forms part of his intuition, and later decisions. Common core values will inevitably strengthen the leader's team, and his success through it. At the same time his personal value system will, over time, and through his influence over key appointments and example, ripple downwards to affect the companies culture. The leader's intuition thus becomes an unconscious test, not just of personal rapport, but of cultural fit.

Role visualisation

But what further thinking power does the leader call upon to determine whether a person will fit the role and the culture? In practice, as we saw in Chapter 2, the leader has to *imagine* the individual in his or her role and different scenarios in order to get a feel for whether they will fit. In thinking terms, the leader 'pictures' the person handling a difficult client, holding their own in a board meeting, handling the press and so on. This is another high-speed operation of the creative right brain, so can be carried out exhaustively, if largely unconsciously, during the otherwise 'conscious' questioning of the interview.

Not surprisingly, people who are known to be good visualisers – able to construct clear future scenarios mentally – turn out to be good judges of people, and certainly are very familiar with the initial chemistry we have discussed. So, once again, right brain ways of thinking are called upon when quality insight is required. And it turns out that, because the other more rational and controllable aspects of the selection can be well catered for by good professional staff and systems, the vestigial responsibility of the leader comprises almost wholly this imaginative, intuitive, and largely subconscious personal judgement. This is where the value is added.

INTUITION AND PROFESSIONAL RECRUITMENT

None of this is to suggest that such mystical powers are just for the mega managers. Intuitive thinking happens all the time, at every level. It just becomes more obvious as decisions are filtered upward, and the manager, at any level, has to add something extra to the process. But the experience of the chief executive of a large staff recruitment company seemed to put all this into perspective. The company hired outside consultants to work with their own recruitment specialists to standardise the interview process, with a view to best practice and consistency. A lot of time and money was invested, and the new systems were eventually implemented. Before long, however, their company offices were inundated with calls from irate clients whose recruits had turned out to be a disaster, or had not been properly matched with the job and the company. The outcome was that the whole new scheme was abandoned, and the recruitment company reverted to its former practice of allowing professional interviewers wide discretion in making choices. Intuition – the very chemistry that the top managers, sometimes unknowingly, experienced and which, only with hindsight, had been an important part of the group's recruitment success – was now officially recognised. 'Chemistry' had earned credibility as a vital part of the professional recruitment process.

Of course, chemistry works in two directions – liking or disliking tends to be mutual, and an interviewee might be just as keen to bring an interview to an early close as the interviewer. David Webster, deputy chairman at Argyll, met (now chairman) Sir Alistair Grant in a pub when he (David) was 28 years old. On the strength, it seems, of personal chemistry alone, David gave up a promising career in finance to work for this 'lunatic' who offered him a job (only to learn that he offered just about everybody jobs). But the instant chemistry has stood the test of time and rocketed David Webster to a position of top leadership, through the enduring partnership. In another case the risky appointment of a 16-year-old – on a whim, or pure hunch – provided not just an eventual finance director, but, some 40 years of successful partnership later, a successor to the top seat.

LEADING TOP TEAMS

Team working did not feature a lot in my discussions with leaders, with some important exceptions. Whilst figuring highly in any study of empowerment, organisational development, or management generally, the leadership aspects of team working are more specific. The immediate team, the board of directors, formed the main team with which the leaders were directly involved – at least in their role as company leader. But given some open lines of discussion, including the obvious 'what makes a good leader', it was interesting that the subject did not rank higher. Having said that, the choice of immediate team weighs as high as just about any other factor in the leader's role. This was seen and discussed, not from the point of view of team management models, but rather in terms of the interpersonal skills we have seen, and particularly the intuitive aspects. Whilst values might be common, the process of personal chemistry resulted in the wildest differences of personality, style and temperament – as is often the case in the most successful marriages. So the 'balanced team' theory – with differences rather than similarities providing the synergy – is well supported by intuitive judgement in the selection process.

Success on the part of the leader happens, however, not as a result of him or her following a particular theoretical model of team selection and management, but rather as a result of his or her instinctive people skills – the ability to make sound judgements about integrity and fundamental values, about roles and long-term relationships. It involves heart as well as head.

EMPOWERING PEOPLE FOR RESULTS

Real power comes from giving it to others who are in a better position to do things than you are. Yesterday's leaders exercised power through position, knowledge and authority; the individual was often disempowered or ignored. Today's leader depends on a willing following of people. Most of the leaders I met readily attribute their success to others –

usually their immediate colleagues, but often the thousands, or tens of thousands of others who make up the real business. And whilst sometimes these generous acknowledgements have a tinge of the cliché or false modesty, it is hard to imagine a true leader who has not learned the secrets of understanding people, and getting the best out of them.

This is not to suggest that top leaders are people-people – stereotypical extroverts. Many I met tend towards the introvert end of the scale, but nonetheless have enough of the essential people skills to do a highly professional job, and in some cases exercise greater overall leadership skills than their more up-front, demonstrative counterparts. And even if, for some, forays to the coal face of the business are few and contrived, in every case the leader depends heavily on other people – not least the close team of directors.

Empowerment fits well into the leadership patterns we found. There are, however, some not-too-convincing clones of empowerment that have to be eliminated if we are to avoid the expensive mistakes that some companies have made, trying any buzz idea on offer that promises to solve their problems. Empowerment, for instance, is sometimes confused with delegation. Delegation was always a management requirement, and a classical part of leadership, but the several tiers of management that fuelled delegation have largely disappeared. Large corporations with more than a handful of management tiers have either gone through the trauma of delayering, or are now in the process of doing so. Those which have not are either fortunate monopolies, not subject to market forces, or living on the fat of easier times, but vulnerable now to more lean competition. But delegation, without also giving authority and exercising trust, is unlikely to get the level of motivation and results you are after. Delegation, all too often, means dumping–workload, rather than power, is transferred, and no natural 'followership' is created.

Just as tempting as delegation is the passing down of responsibility and accountability. But giving responsibility without the authority needed to exercise it is no better than dumping. Further, without the necessary skills and competencies, staff will not be equipped to take on their new responsibility. The leader with insight sees things from a people rather than an organisation perspective. Instead of pushing tasks and accountability down the organisation, individuals are trained, supported and trusted to get on with what they are capable of doing. Empowerment has also been confused with the cost-cutting and delayering of management that has usually taken place in parallel, with all the fear and lack of trust that accompanies it – hence the very negative connotations of the word itself in some companies. People are not stupid. They know when they are being used for short-term profits or as pawns in a bigger game. Cost-cutting and redundant management is one consequence of many years of skewed power. Empowering people at the front line helps to put the power where it works best.

Sharing power

So empowerment should not be confused with delegation, responsibility, or cost-cutting. Rather, it is about sharing power, in such a way as to increase the chances of fulfilling the company's goals. It involves, for example:

- sharing information about how the company is performing

- sharing rewards among those who achieve that performance

- sharing the knowledge that employees need to fully carry out their jobs; and, most importantly

- sharing power to make the necessary decisions.

All of this fits well the values and qualities we found in leaders at the top. Keeping in touch with staff seems to create the 'followership' that leadership is all about, provided the leader values and respects his people, and is not just performing a chairman's or CE's duty. The very process of listening and gaining knowledge – keeping in touch in a wider sense – adds to the essential rapport upon which leadership depends.

Harnessing the total person

There is a parallel between the way we have looked at the leader, and the way the empowering leader regards his people. Some of the key characteristics of the top leader, as we have seen, are not confined to his role as a business chief, within whatever office hours he works, and to the confines of the office, plant or retail store. But they concern the leader as a total person, and thus embrace his values, beliefs and non-business interests. In the same way, empowerment can only start when each employee is seen in such a light – as a total, unique person, with a life that goes beyond the company. Paradoxically, some of the best contributions of the leader stem from outside his direct role. And the real creativity of the employees is only tapped when they are also recognised and treated in this holistic way.

It was generally agreed among the leaders I talked with that there is an enormous waste of talent within companies, and that individual workers do not bring to bear the enthusiasm, motivation and creativity they might apply to a sport or hobby. Brains seem to be left at the clocking-in machine. Yet a blinkered, unproductive worker can be transformed on a Friday afternoon and be let loose to engage in all kinds of creative, fulfilling pursuits. A British Rail train driver, for example, is mayor of a local authority corporation – a corporation with the complexity of a sizeable business, and requiring a reservoir of energy and creativity that might be lost to a nine-to-five employer. A quiet book-keeper masterminds the village fete, coaches young athletes, or sits on a school board of governors. Somone remarked to Len Simmonds, then MD of T Bailey Forman, that 'everything would be fine if they were all like the MD' – referring of course to his motivation and creativity, and passion for the business. Some companies are focusing specifically on releasing the creativity of their staff. When putting his vision to the staff of Tesco in 1992, David Malpas, managing director, said he wanted them to 'think, become more imaginitive, invent more, be different.'

So leaders, in a very real way, have to share their passion, enthusiasm, and whatever drives them. Len's vision is no less than total empowerment – in his case, 500 people thinking about the business. This is one of today's biggest business challenges, and is clearly what will mark out the effective leader.

Reshaping the organisation

If we want to reinvent the corporation, we have got to assert human capital – people – as its most important strategic resource. A start has been made; companies, for example, are now interested in the health of their staff. They are concerned about smoking, and try to encourage exercise, a healthy lifestyle and the reduction of stress. Not many years ago all this would have been considered an intrusion into personal privacy. Now it forms part of corporate strategy, not a revival of Victorian philanthropy. This time it is a recognition that human beings will make or break a company.

The empowerment movement is pragmatic in other ways.

There has been a massive whittling away of middle management. Whole tiers have disappeared in the move towards flatter organisations and cost reduction. Effective delegation now means the release of authority as well as the giving of responsibility. It involves trust and empowerment on the part of managers, and the risk that accompanies it – it demands true leadership. Technology and economic recession have added to this reshaping of organisations, but the key is in how people are empowered. Hierarchies are being replaced by self-managing structures of various kinds, networks, multi-disciplinary teams and small groups. Companies just starting out are more likely to start with flat structures in which people, in effect, manage themselves. Computers are replacing middle managers at a faster rate than robots are replacing assembly-line workers. So more is expected of staff at a lower and lower level. People have got to be given the power to produce the results.

But external factors such as technology and economic recession might hide the reality: that people are more productive when they are valued highly and trusted. Sadly, this reality has not been put to the test on any great scale. There is more lipservice than devolved power and trust. When it comes to real empowerment, we are in uncharted waters. Having hardly come to terms with a participative style of management, and still reeling from the inconsiderate customer being king, the empowerment ideal is a big one to grasp. Every employee might now be afforded a central place in the overall success of the enterprise – a stake. The leader is the architect of this process; some spoke with passion about what is possible when people are tuned in to the company's goals.

As empowerment becomes more than the rare exception, another new phenomenon will play a part. Good people will increasingly be attracted to those firms which can give them the freedom and fulfilment they want. Competition will no longer be just to do with financial rewards – if it ever was. So the leadership we are describing will no longer be an added extra; given a choice, people will exercise it, and follow the leader that values and empowers them.

Training as we know it will have to accommodate change on an ever-increasing scale. During the Second World War the army taught illiterate recruits to read in six weeks. With learning technology we can match and surpass that. But we need to be clear about what we want of our people. Releasing creativity, helping personal growth and fostering a collective vision will rank higher than external skills, which tend to be rapidly acquired in any case when motivation and self-image are right. But creativity and self-image cannot be trained in the conventional, technique-based way to which we are accustomed. The message of *Think Like a Leader* has been more about the leader *inside* – his attitude and lifestyle – than his adherence to models and techniques. And the same intuitive, holistic approach applies equally to the leader's managers and staff. This is the way to empowerment.

Creating the culture

Empowerment has only worked where the culture of an organisation encouraged it – where the climate was right. If people share a common set of goals, and a common perspective on how to achieve them, and speak a common language that enables them to work together, they will tend to do well despite the organisation structure. This is not to say that organisation and structure do not play a part. There are things you can do that *support* an empowering culture, but these are unlikely *create* one. For example, you can:

- break a business into groups, by customer, product, or whatever

- take out layers of the hierarchy which will not be needed as power moves downward

- remove systems and functions that do not help achieve the goals of the business in its empowered form

- move support services from the corporate centre, or even from the top of a profit centre structure, to the front line

- make your communication and systems flow across the operations rather than up and down.

Each of these will move power, and tend to affect 'how we do things around here' – the culture. But conversely, without an enabling culture any such organisational changes are likely to fail. At worst, there needs to be a *desire* at the top for cultural change for the better. And that is where the leader comes in, both in fostering the values, whilst having the power to create and demolish structures and systems when needed.

British Rail carried out a major restructuring to reflect their many separate businesses, each of which has tended to take on its own cultural identity. In this case the sheer size and complexity of the operation required a new structure to form the foundation of the many changes that had to come, including market focus and commercial performance measurement. The structure was in parallel with clearly defined business goals which also added to the cultural identity of the staff. This is one of the few cases where restructuring seemed to precede a cultural change. In fact, it was part of a fundamental change in thinking that came right from the top.

But even new structures and systems that make sense cannot be imposed. You simply cannot enlist staff by redesigning systems or changing reporting lines. Even if you win an employee (a legal servant), you will not get the 'total person' working for you. You have got to win hearts as well as minds. So this mysterious culture has to come from the top. Although individual members of staff, even below manager level, might create cultural pockets around them – resulting in sometimes remarkable creativity and output – they are unlikely to affect the whole organisation. Yet a change at the top has been known to bring about a major shift in culture in a relatively short space of time. That is where the people-power lies; that is where the leverage is – not just in terms of authority and position power, but in terms of example, and role model of the leader. People learn to 'read' the boss. His or her values and beliefs are anticipated and to some extent emulated by the immediate team, who get to know the boss's preferred way of getting things done. Those with very different values are likely to lose out in any reshuffle, so leaving the remaining value culture to perpetuate and trickle downwards.

Managers reporting to directors will use the same anticipatory instincts, thus strengthening and spreading the cultural ethos. If the boss praises initiative, they will start doing so. If the boss encourages risk-taking and allows mistakes, old fears will start to be overcome. And so on, throughout the organisation. The stronger the vision and beliefs of the leader, the greater will be this cultural impact. A leader who values people as individuals very highly will create a culture that is open to creative, empowered staff. The process is reinforced each time an appointment is made from outside the company. A top manager might well bring an entourage along – again more than likely sharing similar broad values – and this can speed up the cultural impact of the leader. But any outward appointee will have to pass the 'chemistry' test of the leader, as we saw earlier. This intuitive process seems to further support the values of the leader, and so will strengthen the cultural basis that he or she is creating – often unknowingly.

Empowering from the top

Some of the companies claiming a high level of empower-ment, with results to support it, follow just this pattern. Somebody – a person, the leader – brings about the winning culture. This is easy to spot when the chief is the original founder and entrepreneur, but it can also be seen when an outsider comes in. Typically the process is very slow, and for this reason a leader has to be on board for some time, espe-cially in a large group, before he can expect to influence its culture. This is particularly so where staff turnover is slow, and an existing board stays intact. But on some occasions the change can be as quick as a couple of years. Either way, this is the leadership route to empowering people. An auto-cratic boss can certainly make an impact, but will not reach the hearts, and certainly will not unleash the creativity in the company. Such a boss might get the short term results that often accompany a fear-rather-than-fun culture. Similarly, a non-intuitive super-analytical manager will have neither the vision nor the vital intuitive skills that we have met throughout this book. That something that leadership calls for will be missing.

When Len Gerstner took over as boss of IBM, his prior-ity, understandably, was 'the financials'. Facing a stifling corporate culture, and losses running into billions of dol-lars, an internal survey of 1,200 top managers confirmed that 40 per cent still did not accept the need for change. Gerstner shook staff to the core by replacing the three 'basic beliefs' upon which the Watson family business had been based – pursuing excellence, providing the best customer service, and showing employees respect as individuals. In the eight goals that replaced the three, respect for the indi-vidual dropped to number eight. Among other things, the new values included the importance of employees seeing themselves as 'owners'. But, as one wrote in a newsletter,

'Nice try, Len, but it's hard to think as owners when we are treated as hired hands.' IBM has been a case study in the effect of a culture, and the impact of the early leaders on that culture. It remains to be seen what changes the present leadership will make, after the obvious and necessary cutbacks. What is certain is that the leader's role in creating and changing a culture, and empowering staff, will turn out to be crucial.

Not only has empowerment to be the real McCoy if it is not to degenerate into an expensive corporate joke or eliminate whatever respect already existed for the leader, but it has to start at the top. Repeatedly, in studies of corporate excellence, a culture that has spawned impressive results has been traced back to a leader. In some cases such a figure is obviously charismatic, but in far more cases may have been little known outside the business. This leader's impact is more subtle, but nonetheless powerful. But in each case the power of example is greater than that of edict. And beliefs and values seem to be far more important than personality or outward management style. A genuine belief in the individual is readily communicated. Integrity and vision on the part of the leader, and the respect for and trust in the people cannot be measured in terms of material reward. It is another part of leadership that you can't fake. And that is what true empowerment is about. Like customer care, and continuous quality improvement, it goes far deeper than structures, systems and even skills. It involves the human psyche, of which the successful leader is an ardent student.

Levels and scope of empowerment

Whilst starting at the top, the leader has to shift power at different levels. Most attempts at empowerment are too limited, tinkering with something that is as fundamental as the business itself. There is a critical mass that applies when a culture has to change, and this affects the success of any intervention aimed at empowering.

Leaders can usually empower the odd self-starter who already exercises initiative and good judgement. This does not require a great leap of faith and trust – lots of number twos have taken on a lot of power, having proved themselves over a period to grateful bosses. But to empower a whole team whose individual members vary in skills, judgement and creativity, and even loyalty, requires boldness and trust. So the idea of empowering the whole organisation really does require a special kind of leadership. It is a high-risk, high-reward people strategy. And at this level, it is an *idea*. The practical outworking of any empowerment ideal is at the individual and team level. So as a leader you have to be aware of these levels – individual, team, and organisation. Your greatest power is with your immediate colleagues and your own team. The CEO's power is mirrored in his directors, who lead their own functional or business teams – and so on throughout the organisation. Visions and values are thus shared, and the teams add synergy to the goal-achieving process.

As well as understanding these levels, the leader also has to be aware of the kind and degree of empowerment that is right for the organisation – and in particular the degree of discretion that can be given to different individuals. This became very apparent in my discussions with a number of retail chains which more or less replicate successful operations at each store. Some businesses work to very tight operating boundaries, perhaps in the form of successful marketing or production systems, or are tied to a specific technology. Similarly safety standards or a regulatory framework might reduce the degree of individual initiative, even in the most enlightened business.

The scope of an individual's job, therefore, will vary in its knowledge and skills base, the discretion over what tasks can be carried out, the discretion over when and how they can be done, and the degree to which an individual can influence policy or affect operations outside their own area of work. All of this will differ from company to company and industry to industry, so a standard empowerment model is no more likely than a leadership one. Given the right leadership and the ripple effect of a culture which values people, each of these potential obstacles to empowerment is readily surmountable.

Working for fun

The extra output of empowered people is not directly related to financial rewards. Even routine work can be fun if employees are convinced that it matters – for example, volunteers can happily spend hours licking stamps in a fund-raising campaign for their favourite charity. They will put lots of time and energy into all kinds of out-of-work activities that bring no money reward, but that provide the self-fulfilment and motivation which nourishes on a different kind of inner reward system. In the few, special cases where a large company has a positive, customer-focused culture, performance seems to improve. Where work is fun, miracles of performance can happen.

A lot of the leaders noticed that more ideas are likely to be got from staff during social, or semi-work situations than through any nine-to-five processes – exactly reflecting their own out-of-office creativity. Archie Norman puts a lot of emphasis on social activities – again recognising that he is dealing with people with 24-hour lives and non-work interests, who tend to respond when so valued. All kinds of sports and other activities are sponsored by Asda. On a Friday staff can come to work in any kind of clothes, provided they wear the George brand (Asda's own); in their open culture the 'George on Friday' option is readily taken up. This capitalises on the 'Saturday morning culture' that many companies are familiar with, and the unwritten rule that casual dress is expected. On these occasions staff often go the extra mile in unpaid work, tending to be at their most creative and productive.

Bryan Drake, MD of Servowarm, also fosters social events and sees company benefits. A late-night conversation with two inebriated service engineers at a social function revealed some home truths about a bonus scheme which resulted in big changes and an improvement in sales results.

Informal evening sessions at Sainsbury's bring David Quarmby a wealth of ideas and feedback as staff feel valued and tend to be relaxed, highly motivated and creative. Besides being a listener, the leader also needs to create a climate in which staff are free to express opinions and ideas without risk of ridicule or censure. This is a big part of the leader's role. Leaders themselves have wide interests and can appreciate the diversity of talent and knowledge that staff can bring into their companies. They know that their only real power is the power of their people.

Untapped resources

Len Simmond's vision of all his people thinking about the business is something that Asda has begun to experience. Some 7,000 ideas and suggestions came from staff in 1993 as part of an ongoing policy of involving and empowering the staff. Every one of those suggestions was considered, and many have resulted in changes in every part of the business. Although the commercial value – the real bottom-line benefits of all that previously untapped creativity – is very significant, Archie Norman is not concerned only with this aspect of the open, empowering culture he is creating. Valuing and empowering the staff is even more basic than the profit drive. The same empowering process creates the high morale and open, creative culture on which quality, customer service and innovation – the very success of the business – depend. Profit *follows* a sound people strategy.

The way that staff can help the business in ways far outside their official job functions illustrates the power of this untapped resource. Some plastering work at T Bailey Forman was done with excellence by a skilled cake-icer. A cleaner came up with an idea to get rid of pigeons that would cost a few pounds rather than the estimated £5,000. A potholing enthusiast at Nuclear Electric saved the company £3.5 million (according to an account in their internal newspaper Nuclear Times under the heading 'Pots of Money Saved by Kevin'). Kevin squeezed his slender frame into a tight spot in Hinckley Point B reactor hall to save a top-performing 'outage' (shutdown repair) team some ten days' work – and into the bargain enabled the outage record to be broken. The same staff newspaper reported an energy-saving idea that clocked up savings of £40,000 a year. A shift manager at Shell UK found a way to use otherwise redundant filters and saved £10,000 for the refinery, receiving an Award for Excellence for his actions. So, as far as creativity and innovation is concerned, a company can indeed have 500, or 50,000 MDs – empowered people who can and do make a contribution to the business, drawing on their unique experience and skill, rather than within the confines of their formal role in the organisation.

Getting the best out of people is a number one task of the leader. And it starts with placing a more or less infinite potential value on each person, recognising their uniqueness. It then involves creating a climate in which these powers are freely harnessed, then activating the different hot buttons that unlock all that creativity. John Conlan at First Leisure also tries to foster a 'can do' attitude in all his people. John Hoerner at Burtons stresses the importance of getting across positive messages. He wanted an important project carrying out in about ten days which really should have taken three times as long. He painted a vivid word picture of the finished result, and all the benefits it would bring to the executives involved and the company. He then outlined what was required in very positive terms, avoiding the killers 'shouldn't' 'don't' and 'can't', at the same time giving lots of freedom for the job to be done in the way the managers chose. And, sure enough, a miracle was accomplished.

Getting the picture across

As a leader, somehow you have got to reach your people, to share your vision and capture hearts and minds. As well as using more obvious communication skills, you need to share something you have actually visualised, so that it comes across clearly. Great corporate missions have floundered on poor communication. Being able to 'get the picture across', which demands right as well as left-brain skills, along with giving the freedom to get on with a task, opens up the unlimited resource that your people represent. Clem Jansen asks the question: 'Can you see it happen?' David Moore at BICC Transmitton became known as evangelistic because of his belief in the product. He says: 'You can easily sell an idea to a colleague once your own mental picture is clear.' If you can see it happen, you have a vision to communicate.

There are enormous dangers in words and ideas like empowerment. Too many apparent panaceas have been disappointing or even counterproductive, only to be replaced by other seemingly more sophisticated business school solutions. And because you can't be seen to disagree with the patent wisdom of empowering your people, everybody claims to be doing it (many claiming to have been doing it for years). Some don't believe it, as is seen by their behaviour over a period, yet pay the necessary lipservice. Others convince themselves they are enlightened employers, use the jargon, and apply the systems and structures, but are exposed by their results – the staff morale, ambient culture and company performance. You know when staff are empowered by walking through an office, plant or shop – no matter what you read in annual reports and in framed state-ments in the corridors. Or ask a customer. With all his or her creative brainpower, the leader still has to have power with people.

TIPS FOR TOMORROW'S LEADERS

1. Remember your first impression – how you feel about the person – when meeting someone for the first time. Keep this impression tucked away for future reference. Don't use this as the sole factor in any decision.

2. Try *not* reading a CV and other documentation until after you have met an interview candidate, so you do not form opinions based on what you read. Consider the supporting data along with your face-to-face impressions.

3. Don't over-prepare for an interview. Allow some ques-tions to come to you intuitively in response to what you feel, or a comment they make. You should have all the important facts in writing anyway, so don't waste time on nonsense questions.

4. Note how a candidate relates to others – e.g. your secre-tary, a subordinate, or the tea lady. This may be easier if you hold a lunch or dinner interview in an informal setting. Valuing people highly is fundamental to good leadership, but it might be faked in the formal interview.

5. When choosing someone for your immediate team, see

whether they share your values. Imagine them in different situations – handling difficult people, tackling ethical issues, or being frank with people.

6. Go for someone who can challenge you, and who brings a unique contribution to the team. Avoid clones or yes-men. Aim for variety. Always go for someone better than yourself – that's a feature of true leadership.

7. Don't expect to get the credit for your ideas. Take pleasure in seeing somebody else carry on the torch of your idea. Share your vision.

8. Use out-of-work occasions to keep in touch and create rapport.

9. Be open to ideas and suggestions. Scrap suggestion schemes that do not work. Act on good suggestions or give feedback.

10. Recognise staff achievement of any kind – perhaps in the staff magazine.

11. Avoid killer words like 'can't' and 'don't'. Communicate in a positive way, and expect a lot from your people.

12. Promote and sponsor social events and activities without expecting short-term company benefits. Start investing in your people.

13. Use MBWA to foster initiative, creativity and risk-taking.

14. Acknowledge failure positively where there has been effort and commitment. Do not punish proper initiative, even when it doesn't come off. Publicise some of your own mistakes.

15. Offer training and self-development outside the immediate job function.

16. Treat every member of staff as a leader in the making.

8

Leading in Tomorrow's World

THE KEY DIFFERENCES that mark out leadership are in the way the leader thinks. This is thinking in the broadest sense, which we have seen is largely intuitive and unconscious, and as much to do with attitudes and beliefs as with what we might term intellect. But the aspiring leader can take heart – better thinking does not depend on brain hardware, but is to do with the way we use our fairly standard brain resource. Much of the vital work of the mind happens below the level of consciousness, and is *not* helped by trying. So whilst seeming to expend much effort, a rational, logical, cerebral manager may not produce the results that a more natural leader, thinking holistically, produces.

However, this openness to intuitive, creative thought, and the wide perspective demanded at the helm of an organisation, is also linked to the leader's lifestyle. The lessons I drew from the leaders did not involve new techniques or theories. But a pattern was apparent to do with how they think and the way they live, and simple enough for any of us to recognise and apply.

We have seen how intuitive thinking skills can help the leader in just about every aspect of the role. In problem-solving and decisions, for example, some of the stages in the thinking process involve the right brain. Usually intuitive

188

feelings are an ally of logic and reason, resulting in what we call common sense. The 'logic' of a spontaneous good idea is worked 'backwards', so the intuition is given credibility. In the cases where we are 'in two minds', the subconscious mind is giving us – free, gratis – a *warning* based on a few billion of our own experiences which we are not capable of handling at a conscious level. In choosing people – another 'must' for leaders – these intuitive powers come into their own even more, as we are in a highly subjective world involving subtle interpersonal communication and personal 'chemistry'.

Then in all kinds of situations the visualising prowess of the right brain enables us to see scenarios and test them out, bringing extra perception, with lightening speed, into decisions and predictions. When it comes to working out a longer-term vision of the future, the leader is further dependent upon these mystical but awesome powers.

The Nobel prizewinning work of Roger Sperry, and the remarkable developments in neuro-physiology since then, have exposed a long preoccupation with the dominant left brain hemisphere, and the narrow concepts of intelligence and human behaviour that followed in its wake. This new awareness has been slow to penetrate management 'science', and it is not surprising, although ironic, that our best practitioners of the art of business leadership have been sceptical about the supremacy of analysis over the years. Sadly, they had no articulate defence. How do you argue a gut feeling? How do you subject an intuition to laboratory testing? And how does the mute right brain fight its corner against the articulate, post-rationalising left brain?

The extraordinary response of top leaders to our research, and the barrage of affirming experience revealed in the interviews, simply adds to the convincing work of Sperry and the popularising campaigning of Edward De Bono (of lateral thinking fame) and Tony Buzan in human creativity. The weight of evidence and awareness of the importance of the right brain, however, is not enough. Most managers remain unaffected. What we know has to be communicated to the heart as well as the mind. And what we think has to be translated into what we do.

I have suggested that lifestyle and attitude can stimulate and harness the kind of thinking associated with leaders and good managers. This emerged from my discussions with the leaders as repeated anecdotes and simple principles, and these are scattered throughout the book. As we have seen, the stories spill outside the office and business into evenings and weekends, and involve the whole life, night and day, of the leader. It remains for me to marshal these into an easily remembered shortlist that makes sense to the manager who seriously wants to go along the path of excellence and leadership.

A PATTERN OF LEADERSHIP LIFESTYLE

The lives of the leaders varied a lot, and, as recognised at the outset, they tended to be 'their own person'. In a true thinking sense, each person is unique. But there was something of a pattern in the lifestyle that was associated with the intuitive thinking and creativity that seem to mark out the leader. As interview followed interview, the common factors became more apparent – even the anecdotes took on familiar themes. The pattern that emerged embraced all the skills the leaders saw as important, from solving problems to choosing people. So it applied to just about all the leaders I met, in just about all the areas of leadership we covered.

Managers find it hard to accept simple solutions, especially when they have lived with the problems they address for years. But that is a mental barrier that has to be crossed, as the very essence of leadership is the ability to simplify the most complex issue, and so see things clearly. The good news is that, unlike the thought processes we unlock, simple lifestyle and attitude changes are easy to understand. You know what you have to do. And you don't need a genetic transplant. Because we are creatures of habit, of course, the simplest of changes can seem hard – especially when they run counter to the high-speed, activity-based life we are so familiar with. Thinking like a leader means living like a leader. They don't all get it right, but we can learn from those who do it best.

Relaxation

The various occasions when creative 'quality' thinking occurred were associated with relaxing times. Because one man's relaxation is another man's stress, this life rule could not be applied to *activities* as such, and nor, for example, to the time of day. Creative thinking when driving the car, for instance, applied to 'natural drivers' who could drive on 'autopilot', and did not need to use highly conscious thinking in the driving process. Provided they did not have an unreasonable deadline, and chose an appropriate route, a long drive could be a genuinely relaxing time, packed with creative thinking. Similarly, getting away from the office reduced the tension of immediate problems and deadlines. Whilst not as fully relaxed as when lying on your back, this state of mind in which freewheeling thought seems to thrive requires a *degree* of relaxation. Mild exercise, or 'doing more than one thing at once' (like driving with the radio on) can actually help the process, as the left brain (Timothy Gallwey's self 1 we saw earlier in the book) is diverted, leaving the right brain to do its own creative thing. Walking, gentle jogging, or other forms of exercise that can be done 'without thinking' help us achieve this degree of relaxation.

A lot of discipline may be required to change long-standing habits and introduce more relaxing times. And attitude is important. So, for instance, travelling time or apparent delays should not be resented, or scheduled out of your life. Squeezing out private space and free thinking time is an insidious feature of modern management. As with any change of habit, this will require practice. But once you are aware of the benefits – the positive outcomes – it is easier to start changing.

Initially you can simply treat times when you do relax as opportunities to think, solve problems, and come up with good ideas. But you can also extend your times of relaxation, or practise specific relaxation techniques. There are plenty of books on this subject, and the benefits for both body and mind have long been recognised. My book *The Right Brain Manager* covered relaxation, including how to induce the slow alpha brainwaves associated with creative thinking, and techniques for getting rid of 'busy' thoughts. As well as achieving a better quality of life and health, this 'easy' way of life will also promote leadership qualities.

Private, uninterrupted space

Most of the examples of what appeared to be right brain, creative thinking quoted by the leaders seemed to take place at times when they were either on their own, or at least had a measure of 'private space'. Many listed private space, linked with self-understanding, as a key factor in their total success. So, for example, sitting anonymously in a hotel lounge or an airport would qualify, as would a car or train journey. This explained why the office itself can be so sterile, as it usually affords little privacy.

But privacy, or even anonymity, is not all there is to it. Even when alone for a period of time, if the leader expects to be interrupted at any time, the creative brain is unlikely to do its best work. This phenomenon has a parallel in the large chunks of time the time management experts say you have to set aside for certain important tasks. In our case the task is thinking, but similar rules apply. But quality rather than quantity of time is what counts. Accordingly, a short private time (say a quick walk round the block, or a retreat to the washroom) can be more productive than a long period that (you know subconsciously) can be cut short at any time by an interruption. Even a short car journey can be of more use than a long plane trip with a business colleague for this kind of thinking. The principle is simple enough. But you will need to work out the detailed implications, for instance in terms of controlling incoming telephone calls, an 'open door' policy, and any part of your life that is handed over to others. This uninterrupted time requirement explains also how, early in the morning or at weekends, when the switchboards are closed, an unproductive office can be transformed into a haven of productivity. It also accounts for all the creativity we find in a private domestic rather than business setting.

You can do something about all this. Simple planning will enable suitable times to be set aside, and activities to be fostered that meet these requirements, but do not demand extra time. So this is a good time management device, in which every minute can be made useful, even though you are relaxed, and you can enjoy what you are doing into the bargain. Even what used to seem like 'doing nothing' is directed to achieving your goals when the right brain is brought into play.

It was remarkable how many extrovert leaders had learned for themselves the importance of private time and, even against their natural tendencies, had incorporated it into their way of life. With more introverted managers, the private space is not a problem, but a welcome way of life.

Even so, they may need to address relaxation, and ensure that private space is used for freewheeling thought rather than mentally labouring over a single issue. Sir Paul Girolami, chairman of Glaxo, knows the value of private space, reserving 10 per cent of all his time to himself, and that is after allowing for family and social, as well as business demands. Others had similar rules, although different degrees of success in applying them. Most saw this aspect of their life as a factor in their overall success.

Pleasure

As we have seen, both relaxation and the feeling of private space brought pleasure for the leaders. And this factor played a big part. Cleaning the car, for example, would be good or bad thinking time depending upon how the task was perceived in terms of pleasure or pain or, as we saw in Chapter 5, work or leisure. The same applied to pastimes and sports. The creative time even on a single jog was related to the pleasurable part of the run. Gardening scored high on creative thinking for some, but low for others, just because of the pleasure factor. A long hot bath for one became a shower for another. The common factor, linked with the relaxation and private space, was pleasure. Right brain thinking is not the kind that hurts. At the extreme, in the form of eurekas and flashes of inspiration, or the vivid imagery of imagined goals, it represents a high order of pleasure.

This underlines the importance of managers building leisure time into their lives, or, more aptly, of *perceiving* what might have been viewed as work in leisure, or pleasurable terms. The importance of perception has been known to be vital from the days of old-fashioned positive thinking and self-talk. With the more recent developments in neuro-linguistic programming we now have specific techniques to bring about these changes. For present purposes it is enough to recognise the perception of pleasure as linked with holistic thinking. You can make a start at thinking like a leader in those activities and at those times when you do find pleasure. Then begin to think about your attitude to less pleasant activities, and thus increase your receptiveness to quality thought. A virtuous circle then comes into play. Greater self-awareness allows you to set priorities about your lifestyle which in turn make for further relaxation, pleasure, intuition, perspective – and greater self-awareness.

Keeping in touch

As we saw in Chapter 6, keeping in touch is not just to do with social interaction, but with feeding the mind with wide and rich data from which quality, intuitive thought is drawn. It concerns the ability to create choices by seeing a situation from many different points of view. The more choices you have, the better the quality of your decisions. This leadership requirement can be accommodated by meeting people of different class and interests, travelling, reading, watching and listening. It reflects a way of life that is curious and ever-learning. Managers need to be aware when they are becoming closeted physically, socially or intellectually. Each person, if honest with himself, will know what areas have to be put right. You can develop a way of life that is hungry for knowledge, and sensitive to many points of view. You can actually enjoy keeping in touch.

So there you have a pattern of lifestyle, a shortlist of 'how to live' rules that will help you to think more like a leader. The tips at the end of each chapter suggest ways in which they can be implemented on a day-to-day basis, in such a way that you don't have too much to do or remember, and your imaginative powers and leadership skills are allowed to blossom naturally. As I said at the outset, the leader tends to be his or her own person. Start doing things your way. Choose when and where to do your best relaxing and thinking. Determine your important values and beliefs so that your thinking is channelled the way you want to go. Develop pleasurable interests and extend your goals. A person who lives like this stands head and shoulders above the crowd, and people will tend to follow.

LEADERS AND ORGANISATIONS IN TOMORROW'S WORLD

What is the significance of this for management science, and leadership? What will tomorrow's leaders be like? The apparent dearth of good leaders is bemoaned in much contemporary writing on the subject. Interestingly, but perhaps ironically, this shortage of real leaders has been accompanied by the growth of management as a 'science', the appearance of a new species of professional manager, and an increasing emphasis on analytical techniques. At the same time some of the functional specialisations, such as personnel (now human resources), marketing, and others have become a big part of the organisational scene, detracting somewhat from the role of 'general' management. Inevitably, corporate leaders have come from these functions – historically, production, sales and finance, although the newer disciplines are now adding to the leadership resource base. It was hard for functional leaders to shed their loyalty and narrow thinking. But functional training is rigorous in its analytical bias, and perpetuates the left brain bias of the education system. So, quite unknowingly, it conditions out of our managers any vestige of intuitive thought and creativity that might be needed for a generalist role, and for top leadership in particular. It certainly does not prepare managers for change and uncertainty, as the experience of recent years has shown.

Functional dominance

This 'functional dominance' in business reflected starkly in the composition of boards of directors (most having a strong functional background), then in turn the CEO promoted from their ranks. It has militated against the right brain qualities associated, not just with creativity and holistic thinking, but with successful leadership. The emerging species of the professional manager promised to fill the gap by creating managers who would shed their functional bias and serve the whole corporation. In practice, management became just another discipline, another function, complete with techniques and systems, but with little sign of the qualities that mark out leaders.

Functional dominance, bureaucracy and inertia in large organisations has its counterpart in the well-researched left brain dominance of the corporate individual – especially managers and functional specialists. It is one phenomenon – companies are just a collection of people. Innovative companies comprise innovative people, and only people can have values and vision. It is surprising, therefore, that so many of our present leaders display intuitive skills *despite* their professional training and conditioning, and the ambient bureaucracy in which most were professionally schooled. More by default than by design, it would seem, these leaders have preserved a bit more of the imagination and sixth sense that many of their contemporaries have lost. Their right brains were not allowed to atrophy, despite all the contrary pressures. And this, as we have seen, is to do with how they live, as well as how they think. Maybe they maintained a lot of outside interests, or a creative hobby, or maybe they were not fully conditioned by the system. One way or another, they have kept in touch, managing to strike a balance between work and leisure, and were not swallowed by a left brain organisation.

Creativity is so rare among the ranks of management that the manager with holistic decision-making and people skills stands out from the crowd without trying too hard. Even a few good ideas, a few good decisions – perhaps about choosing his or her immediate team, or an important investment – will give a manager the edge. The intuitive leader shines in a somewhat grey corporate world.

The leadership archetype

None of this supports the archetypal charismatic, larger-than-life leader image. Right-brain thinking and associated lifestyle do not equate with a big personality, strong ego, or an image. Such leaders do exist – a few in politics and a handful in business – but they account for little in the over-all context of business. Leaders of multi-billion pound or household name companies are bound to be known because of the public part of their role and massive followership. But some of these are unassuming introverts, and I did not meet many with inflated egos. So the archetype is no reflection of today's leader.

Nor does what I found support the concept of the leader as super-manager, with a cold analytical brain but no feelings, the model textbook manager of management science. From the straw poll that our research constituted, few such managers get to run successful companies for long. There is the temptation to install an accountant at the helm during a time of heavy cost control and cutbacks, or financial restructuring, and indeed a lot of power is held by financial experts during such times. For short periods, such leadership might produce the short-term results desired. But without the vision and market understanding of a real leader, the future will be bleak. Nor need there be any conflict between visionary leadership and the reality of economic recession and short-term demands. Top leaders live in the real world, and are measured by real results.

THE PEOPLE DIMENSION

The people dimension in modern leadership was found to be central. The proportion of autocratic, Theory X bosses is far smaller than even a decade ago. Such leaders are dinosaurs in a world of customer care and empowerment. The individual now has instant, 'information super-highway' access to the knowledge that once was the preserve of the leader. Having said this, empowerment, as we saw in the previous chapter, with its clones and derivatives, is little more than a buzz word or platitude in most large companies. Power, it seems, has to be squeezed out of managers – more so at the middle levels than at the top – and that is a slow process with low success rates.

There are pockets of devolution scattered throughout the companies, with self-managing teams, high morale and accompanying productivity. But most devolution has followed the economic necessity of wholesale delayering, rather than the ideal of empowerment. Whether top-down or bottom-up, things usually go wrong somewhere in the middle. Few of the leaders I met would claim to have achieved empowerment on any scale. Most recognise well, however, that this is the direction of the future. Several saw the people dimension – harnessing their inherent skills and brainpower – as the very top of any priority ranking. Tomorrow's leaders will have to know how to choose and use people.

The shift of power

Power is shifting. The power of chief executives and chairmen, especially in the large groups, goes without saying. But the nature of this power is changing as consensus-type management becomes more widespread. It is more to do with the person than their position. The way it is used is changing even more, as authority as well as responsibility is passed downwards. The increasing emphasis on horizontal customer-serving structures and systems, rather than traditional vertical pyramid management, moves the balance of power to *individuals* – individual staff members who add value, and the individual customers they serve. Position in the hierarchy, or functional expertise, is much less a source of power. And there are far fewer positions anyway.

There is a power paradox, however, for the leader. In shedding power he actually gets more. In sharing his vision, he motivates others to help bring it about. In freeing others to use initiative and act creatively to pursue the mission, he harnesses others to implement a dream. As was said of the people in Len Simmond's company: 'If only they were all like the managing director.' When empowered, people become like the MD – and we have seen how anyone can take on the qualities of a leader – the leader is truly multiplying his power through people. So there is a shift of power in leadership, away from autocracy and position, and the power of knowledge, towards the power that comes through others. Tomorrow's leaders will have to be team players with people skills. And the demands are such that they will not be able to compartmentalise their lives into business and non-business – any power will be in the total person. A business leader is a person rather than a job. It demands a way of thinking, believing, and living, as well as a way of doing things.

TWO-SIDED THINKING

Having suggested lifestyle changes that encourage the thinking skills for leadership, let me now focus on some questions raised by Leszek Marcinowicz, Vice President Human Resources, Europe, of Parker Hannifin plc.

What about left brain leaders?

Unfortunately we cannot survey the boardrooms for left brain (or right brain) leaders as we might for chartered accountants, or even introverts and extroverts. Imagine a manager who is extremely analytical, rather narrow in his viewpoints, with little imagination, and not very creative. We might say that he 'cannot see the wood for the trees'. That's a left brain manager in layman's terms, and you might have met such. Such a manager that got to the top (perhaps following the Peter Principle of rising to a level of maximum incompetence) would, in turn, be a left brain leader. Can we identify these reliably?

Popular team-style psychometric models have a creative/analytical axis, so there is plenty of evidence about managers in so far as these instruments are valid. They show, for example, that there is indeed a tendency to left brain (analytical) thinking in the case of managers of various kinds, and functional people. However, these instruments usually try to reflect a *preference*, and not necessarily *actual* behaviour in an organisation. A bureaucracy, however, or a company with a culture of fear, would tend to suppress a creative (right brain thinking) preference. So what happens at weekends, and this may not be captured in the work-based instrument, may be different. The result of all this is that a universal left brain dominance is exacerbated inside an organisation, with its systems and controls. So creativity is the exception rather than the rule. First, because of a general bias resulting from our education and training; and second, from the effect of the organisation.

This applies to managers generally, but what about leaders at the top? I met hardly any leaders to whom I would apply the above 'left brain leader' description. Quite simply, based on the large sample size of the study, there aren't many 'left brain' leaders right at the top. It follows that those that rose from the ranks of predominantly left brain management exercised the intuitive, right brain skills we found in the leaders. Somehow, those with strong left brain dominance did not make it. Other anecdotal evidence tells of left brain thinkers getting to the top (contrary usually to negative signals at the appointment) but not staying there for long.

There was, however, more convincing evidence. There were frequent comments from the leaders I met to the effect that they had *changed* to a more intuitive style of management over a period of years, to match the demands of leadership ('I wouldn't have even identified all this ten or fifteen years ago'; 'I'm slowly getting better at first impressions'). Moreover, these leaders were drawn from the mass ranks of middle managers rather than some hotbed of supercreativity, but had adapted their thinking somewhere along the way. So what about left brain leaders? Still using the layman's description above, they are hard to find at the top in the premier division, or even in far smaller companies. A cursory reading of the earlier chapters will suggest the reasons.

Is it just right brain thinking?

The second question is: 'Are we saying that one key attribute of a successful leader is right brain thinking?' The way we think – holistically or in a sequential, logical way – is more than an attribute or skill, and even more basic than personality type. Right brain thinking, for instance, might apply to an extrovert as much as to an introvert. We abandoned the centuries-old search for characteristics or traits at the beginning. If we ask whether successful leadership is primarily concerned with how a person thinks, and that such thinking includes imagination, feelings, hunches and intuition, the answer to the second question must be yes. But this is no latter-day revelation. 'As a man thinketh in his heart, so he is' is very seasoned wisdom. Behaviour follows thinking (of the heart variety), and performance and leadership success follows from behaviour. Holistic thinking is central to human achievement And yes, this holistic way of thinking seems to be central also to successful leadership.

How can you test for it?

The third question is: 'How can you test for it?' A simple psychometric test was included in my book *The Right Brain Manager*. As it happens, most managers have a good idea of their own bias before they carry out the test. But there are major flaws in this and any such test, which I will address in order to help explain the importance of the final conclusion of the whole study.

First, the two sides of the brain are essentially *two minds*. This is not the place to outline the two-mind theory, based on the Nobel prizewinning work of Roger Sperry, but the very different 'operating systems' in the respective brain hemispheres, and the different kinds of thinking we have met throughout the book, make a convincing case. Every time we say 'I'm in two minds', or have to reconcile 'heart and mind', or logic and feelings, we acknowledge something of our two minds. In so-called split-brain patients, whose interconnecting corpus collosum – joining the two hemispheres of the cortex – was severed, their behaviour suggesting two distinct *persons* were observed, not just two minds in one person. Each hand would fight to choose a different dress from the wardrobe, for example, or one hand would stack cans in a grocery store while the other hand (linked to the other side of the brain) immediately took them down. In a normal human being, the only difference is that the two brains are connected, so we have to *make up our minds* one way or the other, reconciling often conflicting decisions or courses of action. So, in any test, which side of the brain is responding?

If you have completed psychometric tests yourself, no doubt you recall questions which you felt could be answered either way. We all have an intuitive, imaginative side that makes us inherently creative. And we all have a verbal, logical, analytical side that wants to behave in a more 'rational' way. But, more than that, we can switch from one operating mode to the other – getting a bright idea then checking it out – from moment to moment. One moment you are cool and analytical; the next moment your feelings take over. As the left brain has control over language and tends to rationalise all our behaviour (in effect, makes 'excuses' that make sense) we are not too sure 'who' is giving the psychometric responses.

The next problem makes psychometric tests even less useful. On a right-left scale, a person who used five per cent of their left brain, and five per cent of their right brain would (forgetting the first problem of which side responded) finish up right in the middle – a nicely balanced thinker. But a person using 95 per cent of their left brain and 95 per cent of their right would show the very same score – another balanced thinker. However, in the second case we have what we might call a genius, someone who has computer-like logical and analytical powers, yet at the same time great imagination and creativity – an Einstein or da Vinci, perhaps.

Two tests might provide the answer. First, a measure of left brain power, in a similar way to IQ testing, which largely measures just that. Then, in a relaxed mode, when brainwaves are in slow alpha mode, a test of right brain skills that does not depend upon language or numerical ability. Two brains, two tests. And the results would show the bias I think Les Marcinowitz wanted to test for. But would this test for leadership qualities?

YOUR BRAIN PARTNERSHIP

Thinking about tests highlights the importance of both sides of the brain operating *separately*, each with its own unique way of 'thinking', but, at the same time, the importance of both sides working *together*, to 'make up our mind'. This brings me to the main conclusion of the research. I said earlier that I did not find many left brain leaders. But neither did I find many with a strong right brain bias. In the cases where intuition and imagination seemed strong, there was also evidence of strong analytical ability, and a tendency to check out ideas scrupulously. In other words the leaders seemed to have more developed use of both sides of the brain, as against their more junior left-brain biased colleagues.

This became clear very slowly as the research proceeded. One of the early interviews was with Dr Peter Nevitt, then managing director of Cosworth Engineering, who has since retired. Before the interview got underway, he made it clear where his natural thinking style lay. Reinforced by education and rigorous training as a physicist, he placed himself firmly, and unashamedly, in the left brain camp. That was fine, as my research was 'symmetrical' – it could have turned out either way. For all I knew, intuition could have been ruled out completely by top leaders. But as the discussion went on, it became obvious that Peter was both imaginative and intuitive, responsible for a string of innovative successes in his long years with Ford, and more recently with Cosworth, world-renowned for its state-of-the-art automotive engine design. This was first hand experience of a *bicameral* paradox – two brains in operation at one and the same time. And it was to repeat itself again and again. In some cases the leaders did not see themselves as particularly creative, largely because their self-image was of being very rational and analytical, and the two were not supposed to go together. Only further probing, plus the undeniable facts of a track record, made the right brain skills apparent.

Some of the leaders I met were very creative indeed, but lacked left brain analytical skills. Typically these CEOs would depend very heavily on their finance director or other more pragmatic colleagues to balance their crazy imagination and fantastic visions for the future. But these were not the most impressive as leaders. Those that seemed to stand out were the bicameral thinkers, displaying an awesome combination of double-sided thinking power. Although my scope did not include linking leadership with corporate results, in a few cases the link was very clear indeed, with impressive year-on-year growth above the industry norm during the incumbency of the leader.

Thinking like a leader means using more of the *whole* mind. You need to keep every ounce of logic, rationale, prudence, and professionalism, with financial awareness or some solid functional training thrown in. There is no room for seat-of-the-pants entrepreneurs running these vast organisations and commanding the trust of thousands of employees. They can start them up and sell out, make their millions, or lose them. But, as a 21st century business leader, along with your rationale, you need to rediscover your childhood imagination. You need to detect and trust the subtlest intuition, and develop the sixth sense that sees beyond the obvious. You need to call on innate ability to judge people accurately. You need to hone up your visualising powers and use them to start creating your own future, and that of your business.

You can start with how you live. In the tips I have given there is not a discounted cash flow in sight, and you don't have to learn some new computer software. It's all common sense. Everything is within your potential. Visualising is just using your seeing sense internally, and this comes with practice. In time you will experience the future so realistically that it will be as good as achieved. Given such a clear vision, your brain is primed and ready, and will help you along the way cybernetically by presenting associations, ideas, and the odd eureka. You can develop your other inner representation systems in the same way, and become, for example, a better natural listener. You can learn to *feel* more, and be more sensitive, harnessing your body as well as your mind to produce better quality decisions. You will start to recognise and value a gut feeling. As a person, you will become more aware of what is happening inside.

Remember – there's nothing special about leaders, except that they think like leaders.

Index